EXTREME IMAGINATION:
A GUIDE TO OVERCOMING MALADAPTIVE DAYDREAMING

EXTREME IMAGINATION: A GUIDE TO OVERCOMING MALADAPTIVE DAYDREAMING

BY

Kyla Borcherds

Cherish
EDITIONS

First published in Great Britain 2024 by Cherish Editions
Cherish Editions is a trading style of Shaw Callaghan Ltd &
Shaw Callaghan 23 USA, INC.

The Stanley Building, 7 Pancras Square
King's Cross
London
N1C 4AG
www.triggerhub.org

Text Copyright © 2024 Kyla Borcherds

All rights reserved. No part of this publication may be reproduced, stored in a retrieval system, or transmitted in any form or by any means, electronic, mechanical, photocopying, recording or otherwise, without prior permission in writing from the publisher
British Library Cataloguing in Publication Data

A CIP catalogue record for this book is available upon request
from the British Library
ISBN: 978-1-916920-64-4

This book is also available in the following eBook formats:
ePUB: 978-1-916920-65-1

Kyla Borcherds has asserted her right under the Copyright,
Design and Patents Act 1988 to be identified as the author of this work

Cover design by More Visual
Typeset by Lapiz Digital Services

Cherish Editions encourages diversity and different viewpoints. However, all views, thoughts and opinions expressed in this book are the author's own and are not necessarily representative of us as an organisation.

All material in this book is set out in good faith for general guidance and no liability can be accepted for loss or expense incurred in following the information given. In particular this book is not intended to replace expert medical or psychiatric advice. It is intended for informational purposes only and for your own personal use and guidance. It is not intended to act as a substitute for professional medical advice. The author is not a medical practitioner nor a counsellor, and professional advice should be sought if desired before embarking on any health-related programme.

This book is dedicated to two very special people who live in my imagination. Thank you for saving me. I'm glad I trusted you.

CONTENTS

Foreword	xiii
Introduction	xvii
Maladaptive daydreaming is real	xvii
I'm a lifelong daydreamer	xviii
You're not alone	xx
Using this book	xx
Your greatest gift	xxi
Taking back control of your mind	xxii
PART 1 UNDERSTANDING IMMERSIVE AND MALADAPTIVE DAYDREAMING	**1**
1 What is daydreaming?	3
Why do we daydream?	3
Different styles of daydreaming	5
Misconceptions about daydreaming	9
What you daydream about	10
My story	13
Types of vivid narrative daydreaming	15
2 The science behind maladaptive daydreaming	19
How common is maladaptive daydreaming?	20
How is maladaptive daydreaming classified?	21
Diagnosing and treating maladaptive daydreaming	26
3 Why did your daydreaming become maladaptive?	31
Daydreaming is your mind trying to keep you safe	31
Claire's story	33
Maladaptive daydreaming can start at any age	35
Sola's story	37

	An escape not a solution	38
	Are there any taboo daydream topics?	40
	Maladaptive daydreaming can't be viewed in isolation	42
4	How can maladaptive daydreaming harm you?	45
	You waste a lot of time	46
	You don't know how to handle romantic relationships	47
	You don't have many friends	47
	You don't set or achieve goals	48
	You lose your sense of self	49
	You don't mind-wander	49
	You run away from challenging emotions	50
	You keep making the same mistakes	51
	You stay in your comfort zone	51
	You judge yourself for being a daydreamer	51
5	Other conditions that are associated with maladaptive daydreaming	55
	Why do so many maladaptive daydreamers have poor mental health?	55
	ADHD	57
	Depression	60
	Anxiety	63
	You can't address maladaptive daydreaming in isolation	67

PART 2 HOW TO OVERCOME MALADAPTIVE DAYDREAMING — 69

6	Preparing for healing	71
	The four steps to overcoming maladaptive daydreaming	72
	The ultimate goal: immersive daydreaming	74
	Why immersive daydreaming?	75
	What does healthy immersive daydreaming look like?	76

	It's OK to ask for help	78
	The importance of self-monitoring	83
7	Overcoming shame	89
	What is shame?	89
	Why it's important to overcome shame	90
	Why daydreamers feel shame	91
	Being a daydreamer doesn't make you a bad person	95
	How to overcome shame	96
	Challenging the negative beliefs you have about your daydreaming	99
	Sola's story	102
	Beyond shame – learning to like yourself	103
	Two things to do right now	105
8	Understanding why you escape	107
	Daydreaming feels great while you're doing it	107
	Daydreaming as a coping mechanism	108
	What need might your daydreaming be meeting?	111
	What is your daydreaming allowing you to escape from?	113
	The importance of tolerating negative emotions	116
	Therapy to process trauma	117
9	Making real life worth coming back to	123
	You maladaptively daydream because your life is a mess	123
	Address any coexisting problems	127
	Learn to tolerate discomfort	128
	Take a small step toward achievement	132
	Build social connections	135
	Look after yourself	137
10	Taking control of your daydreaming	141
	Keep monitoring your progress	142
	Managing your triggers	143
	Resisting the urge to daydream	145

	Present-moment awareness	147
	Allocating time to daydream	149
	Give yourself rules to follow	153
	Start your day grounded in reality	154
	Daydream relationships	156
11	Bringing it all together	161
	The four steps to overcoming maladaptive daydreaming	161
	How this process changed my life	163
	You have a beautiful life to look forward to	165

PART 3 LEARNING TO LOVE YOUR IMAGINATION — 169

12	Learning to love your daydreaming	171
	What we'll cover in this part of the book	171
	Your daydreaming is different now	172
	Immersive daydreaming is a form of play	174
	Daydreaming can also be useful	174
	Immersive daydreaming is different and beautiful	175
13	Reconnecting with your authentic self	177
	Who is your daydream self?	177
	Why your daydream self can be real	180
	You need to rediscover your authentic self	182
	How to reclaim your authenticity	183
	My journey back to myself	185
14	How your characters can support you in real life	191
	What is a free character?	191
	Connected daydreaming	193
	Chet's story	195
	Why connected daydreaming is helpful	197
15	Use your daydreaming to transform your life	201
	Managing negative emotions	201
	Daydreaming to evoke positive emotions	205
	Daydreaming to increase your confidence	207
	Manifesting and the Law of Attraction	207

The place of peace	211
Sola's story	213
16 Final thoughts	215
How to stay well	215
The benefits of staying well	217
Healing brings peace	219
Let's normalize being a daydreamer	220
Resources	223
To learn more about maladaptive daydreaming	224
Support groups	225
Mindfulness	226
Dialectical behaviour therapy	226
Miscellaneous good stuff	227
The Daydream Place	227
Reference list	229
Acknowledgements	233
Author biography	235

FOREWORD

In 2015, Prof. Eli Somer approached me by email after reading a paper I had written with colleagues about dissociative "absorption and imaginative involvement" and its relevance to obsessive-compulsive disorder. Prof. Somer realized that we were interested in similar things and introduced me to the concept of maladaptive daydreaming, a term I had never heard before, inviting me to collaborate with him. To illustrate the phenomenon, he shared with me (with permission), an email he received from a 50-year-old male suffering from life-long maladaptive daydreaming. This person shared his story with great detail and was very grateful to finally have a name for his condition. I was struck by his eloquent depiction of his unique story, which I still remember years later.

After becoming a maladaptive daydreaming researcher myself, I have also received many emails over the years from maladaptive daydreamers, sharing their stories, volunteering for study participation, and asking for help. Often, they share the moment of revelation that they experienced when they first encountered the concept of maladaptive daydreaming and express how much it meant to them. For us as researchers, these kinds of responses were, and still are, the motivation to continue researching this phenomenon. The lived experience of people with maladaptive daydreaming continues to educate and inspire us in our research. The online communities are what drive this field forward, and they are rapidly growing following people's searches of the internet for a name for their excessive story-weaving.

Such was the experience of Kyla Borcherds. A random thought that popped into her head in 2018 about how she should probably try to "Google" her symptom, led to a life-altering transformation, beginning by realizing that she was not alone and that there was a label for her problem, and culminating, for now, in the writing of this self-help book. In her kind, compassionate, easily readable, and inspiring words, Kyla candidly lays out her own experience and what has worked for her in her journey to overcome maladaptive daydreaming. Her aim in writing this book was to provide other people grappling with this problem with the encouraging guide she wished she herself had been given several years ago.

Kyla has an unusual talent for translating academic knowledge to simple ideas and pragmatic advice, and she utilizes that talent well in this useful book. But other than her writing skills, Kyla has her own experience to draw from. Kyla is not a therapist nor a researcher, but her acquaintance with maladaptive daydreaming runs deep. She has lived experience both in suffering from, and then in healing from, maladaptive daydreaming. Therefore, Kyla is deeply aware of the unique challenges faced by those who are addicted to their compulsive fantasizing and who wish to diminish its hold on them. She is especially acutely aware of the significance and attachment daydreamers feel towards their inner worlds, even if those worlds are hindering their real-world success and perpetuating their loneliness. Consequently, she does not focus only on curbing maladaptive daydreaming, but also on learning to use daydreaming adaptively rather than maladaptively, as promoting, rather than thwarting, one's real-life goals.

Kyla presents a clear perspective on the boundaries between maladaptive daydreaming on the one hand, and healthy immersive daydreaming that can be a creative gift, on the other hand. She also explains to the reader how to get from one to the other through dedicated work and gradual, compassion-filled steps. Kyla's advice to share the experience in online groups coincides with the impression we as researchers have, that these groups act as support resources for individuals with this unrecognized disorder, and this is often a first step for overcoming difficulties associated with maladaptive daydreaming. There are plenty of additional techniques in this book that are very much worth considering. Notably, like any self-help book, this endeavor will not necessarily replace therapy, and those with severe distress, dysfunction, suicidality, etc., should seek professional counselling. However, this useful guide is an easy read that can help a person with moderate levels of distress in starting their journey towards controlling their daydreaming. This book gives labels and structure to what might otherwise be experienced as an overwhelming and confusing process.

Hat's off to Kyla for this wonderful accomplishment, which I'm sure many will find helpful, and I wish the reader a successful journey of changing their habits and exercising their will on their fantastic ability.

Prof. Nirit Soffer-Dudek, Ph.D., Clinical Psychologist
Past President and Director of Research and Science of
the International Society for Maladaptive Daydreaming
Scientific Director of the International Consortium
for Maladaptive Daydreaming Research

INTRODUCTION

What if you had such a vivid imagination that you could create an entire parallel life in your head?

What if you could create fictional characters and love them more deeply than anyone you've ever met in reality?

What if your imaginary world became so compelling that you were willing to sacrifice your career, your relationships and even your health just to spend more time in your fantasy?

What if you became addicted to your own imagination?

Welcome to the world of maladaptive daydreaming.

Maladaptive daydreaming is real

Maladaptive daydreaming is a recently recognized mental-health disorder that's estimated to affect around 2.5% of the population. That's one person in every 40.

The ability to create an imaginary world, populate it with fictional characters and use it as the backdrop to a complex plot that develops over weeks, months or years is a natural trait called immersive daydreaming. It's different from mind-wandering, which is when you have fleeting thoughts about real life – wondering what to have for dinner, looking forward to your next holiday, recalling a conversation you had this morning, etc.

Immersive daydreaming can turn into maladaptive daydreaming if it becomes so compelling that it takes over your life: damaging your career, your relationships and even your sense of self.

Many people, including many mental-health professionals, remain unaware of what maladaptive daydreaming is and how debilitating it can be. Many people doubt that excessive daydreaming can qualify as a mental-health disorder. As a result, maladaptive daydreamers suffer in silence, unaware that their condition has a name and convinced they're the only person in the world who can't silence the stories in their head.

If you've tried to control your daydreaming and found you can't, if you're embarrassed to admit that you're emotionally attached to people who don't exist, or if you're concerned because you thought you would have outgrown this habit by now, this book is for you. I wrote this book to tell you that you're not alone, to validate everything you're experiencing and to show you how to heal from maladaptive daydreaming. And you won't have to give up those characters and worlds that mean so much to you.

I'm a lifelong daydreamer

I first developed maladaptive daydreaming disorder when I was eight years old. A move to a new area had taken me away from my friends. And the children at my new school laughed at my strange accent. I learned that the way to avoid being teased was to say as little as possible. So I suppressed the fun-loving, curious child I'd been, because she no longer felt welcome in the real world. Outwardly, I became quiet and withdrawn. Inwardly, I survived by imagining a world where I could still be myself, where I had friends who accepted me unconditionally and where life was still joyful and exciting. My vivid imagination became my sanctuary.

But over time, it became a prison.

When my life was going well, my daydreaming would fade into the background. It was always there, but I could control it. But when life became stressful, my coping mechanism of choice was to mentally check out. I'd retreat into a fantasy world as a way to avoid reality.

For decades, my daydreaming came and went. There were good times – graduating from university, getting married, becoming a parent. But there were also bad times. Friendships died because I preferred the company of the characters in my head. My career stalled because daydreaming stole my ambition and motivation. When my daydreaming was out of control, I wanted it to stop. When it receded, I missed the excitement of my imaginary world. And through all of it, I kept my daydreaming a secret. I didn't think anyone else had stories bouncing around in their head all the time. And I didn't want to admit that my closest friends existed only in my imagination.

And then one day in 2018, everything changed. I was getting dressed when I suddenly had a random thought that I should google "constantly making up stories in your head". I've always struggled with impulse control, and so two minutes later I was sitting in front of my computer, half dressed, reading an article about maladaptive daydreaming. My life changed in that moment. I finally had a name for the thing I'd been doing all my life. More importantly, I realized I wasn't alone.

Since then, I've learned everything I can about maladaptive daydreaming and its non-pathological equivalent, immersive daydreaming. I've realized that my daydreaming was never the problem. It was how I was using it. I used my daydreaming to escape from anything that felt too painful or overwhelming to face up to. *That* was the real problem. And it was a problem I could do something about.

Six years, a breakdown and a lot of therapy later, I've come a long way. Now my daydreaming is part of how I deal with my problems rather than how I run away from them. Healing from maladaptive daydreaming is possible. I've done it. And by following the strategies in this book, you can do it too – hopefully without the breakdown, and possibly without the therapy.

You're not alone

In this book, you'll meet other maladaptive daydreamers who have faced the same challenges you're facing. You'll learn why your mind works the way it does, what you're using your daydreaming to escape from and how you can turn your daydreaming into a powerful motivational tool that will help you get your life back on track.

Using this book

I've divided this book into three parts.

Part 1 teaches you what maladaptive daydreaming is and how it differs from immersive daydreaming and mind-wandering. We'll look at what the daydreaming experience is like, how it gets out of control and the ways in which excessive daydreaming can harm you. By understanding why your mind works the way it does, you'll be in a much better position to tackle your excessive daydreaming. And by understanding all the different ways your daydreaming is holding you back – which go far beyond the huge amount of time it's stealing from you – you'll be much more motivated to make a change.

In Part 2, I'll walk you through a four-step process for overcoming maladaptive daydreaming. First, we'll address the shame that you feel about not being able to control your daydreaming. Second, we'll look at what you're using your daydreaming to escape from and how to deal with it in a healthier way. Third, you'll learn how to build a real life that's worth coming back to. Once those things are in place, we move on to the final step – directly tackling your excessive daydreaming. Maladaptive daydreaming starts as a coping mechanism, and that means you can't address it in isolation. If you don't want to swap your maladaptive daydreaming for some other (probably equally unhealthy) coping mechanism, you have to address the underlying issue *before* you try to manage your daydreaming.

Finally, in Part 3, we'll look at how you can turn your vivid imagination into your greatest gift. Remember I promised you that you won't have to give up your characters and your worlds? When you have your daydreaming under control, you can do so much more than just enjoy your delicious fantasies. My daydreaming has helped me reconnect with my authentic self, it provided the motivation I needed to pursue some of my biggest life goals, and it saved my life during a suicidal crisis. Overcoming maladaptive daydreaming sets you free to use your imagination to enrich your life.

A NOTE ABOUT THE WORKSHEETS

Most of the chapters in this book (with the exception of Chapters 1, 2, 5 and 16) have an accompanying worksheet, which you can download using the link and QR code provided. After reading each chapter, please take the time to print out and complete the worksheet. It is by completing the worksheets that you'll be able to apply what you learn here to your own life. They will encourage you to do the self-reflection necessary to understand and heal from your maladaptive daydreaming.

Your greatest gift

Let's reframe the questions at the beginning of this section:

What if you had such a vivid imagination that you could create an entire parallel life in your head?

What if you could use your fictional life to inform and empower your real one?

What if you could create fictional characters who become your biggest supporters and most trusted friends?

What if your imaginary world could reconnect you with your authentic self and help you build a life you love?

What if your daydreaming was your greatest gift?

When you overcome your maladaptive daydreaming, all of this is possible.

Taking back control of your mind

That sounds like a big promise, and it is. Overcoming maladaptive daydreaming is going to take more than just reading a book. I can show you the way, but you have to do the work. Change will not be easy. Change will not happen overnight. But if you keep working at it, change will come. And when it does, I promise you, it will be worth it.

This is a pivotal time for maladaptive daydreaming. More and more people are learning about it for the first time. But support for maladaptive daydreamers is not keeping pace with the increase in awareness. At the time of writing, only one academic study into a treatment protocol for maladaptive daydreaming has been published, and the protocol itself has not been made public, because it's the subject of further research. It will be years before science is able to conclusively prove what is, or is not, effective in treating maladaptive daydreaming.

But there are thousands of maladaptive daydreamers, just like you, who can't wait for the science to catch up. You need help now. And in the absence of hard science, you need people like me, and people like the daydreamers featured in this book, to share our experience, to tell you what worked for us and to give you some idea where to start.

Because we're not that different. You probably spent years thinking you were the only person trapped in your imagination. You probably thought you were the only person who needed to pace, or spin, or fidget while you daydreamed. You probably thought you were the only person who didn't have enough willpower to just stop. But you're not. There are thousands of people like you. And if we all share our experience of what works, maybe we can figure this out together.

The strategies I describe in this book worked for me. Similar strategies worked for the people who kindly allowed me to include their stories here. I hope they will work for you.

When I first learned about maladaptive daydreaming, I wished there was a compassionate and comprehensive self-help book that would help me understand my mind and take control of my daydreaming. This is that book.

PART 1

UNDERSTANDING IMMERSIVE AND MALADAPTIVE DAYDREAMING

CHAPTER 1

WHAT IS DAYDREAMING?

You probably picked up this book because you know that your mind goes to places that other people's don't. You have all these wild stories bouncing around inside your head, and for a long time you probably thought that no one else would ever understand. If you've tried to explain it to anyone, you've probably been told that "everybody daydreams". And if you're anything like me, a little voice in your mind would have responded, *"Yes, but not like this!"* The fact is, there are different types of daydreaming. And daydreaming means different things to different people.

Let's begin by looking at what happens when we let our minds run free. Is it true that everybody daydreams? What function does it serve? And does everybody daydream in the same way?

Why do we daydream?

The human mind is rarely, if ever, still. At any given moment, you're going to be thinking about *something*. But frequently, what you're doing doesn't require your full and undivided attention. And in those moments, your mind is free to do its own thing. At its most basic level, that's what daydreaming is: thoughts that are unrelated to what you're doing in that moment.

Daydreaming feels effortless. Your thoughts unfold automatically, without you trying to consciously control them. And that means those thoughts are coming from your subconscious mind. It's as if you've temporarily asked your conscious mind to step aside, and you're allowing yourself to listen to insights that are bubbling up from your subconscious.

That's why daydreaming serves a purpose. The seemingly random connections our minds make while daydreaming are the way our subconscious helps us to understand ourselves, other people and the world around us.

UNDERSTANDING OURSELVES

Daydreaming is an opportunity for self-reflection. We might recall something that happened and wonder why we reacted the way we did. Or we might be deciding between a number of possible options by weighing up the pros and cons. These kinds of thoughts help us understand ourselves better. The content of our daydreams can say a lot about us and what's important to us.

UNDERSTANDING OTHER PEOPLE

When we daydream, our thoughts might turn to the people we know and interact with every day. We might think about how we relate to them and what we could do or could have done to strengthen those relationships. We might mentally rehearse a conversation. And in doing that, we learn that other people are different from us. We learn to see things from their perspective and to understand why they might react differently from us in a given situation.

UNDERSTANDING THE WORLD AROUND US

When we daydream, we let our thoughts wander where they will. And in so doing, we sometimes see connections that we wouldn't otherwise have thought of. Our daydreams are where our subconscious mind explores themes and feelings. They're where we explore "what if –?" scenarios, imagine different possible outcomes and mull over how we'd like life to unfold. If you've ever had a flash of insight or suddenly seen the solution to a problem when you weren't consciously thinking about it, you've witnessed the power of your subconscious at work.

Different styles of daydreaming

You might have read the previous section and thought: *"That's all very well, but how are my daydreams helping me make sense of the world when my daydreams are unrealistic fantasies that have nothing to do with the real world?"* A few years ago, I'd have thought the same. That's because there are different styles of daydreaming.

MIND-WANDERING
What we've been talking about up to now, and what most people mean by "daydreaming", is something that I refer to in this book as "mind-wandering". Mind-wandering is what typically happens when we just let our thoughts go. When we're mind-wandering, our thoughts flit from topic to topic, not settling on anything for more than a few minutes. Sometimes we're not even aware of what we're thinking about. And when something or someone in the real world needs our attention, we can easily snap back to reality.

Mind-wandering might involve recalling a conversation you had, looking forward to the weekend or mentally checking items off your to-do list. Everybody mind-wanders to a certain extent. For a lot of people, it's what happens automatically whenever the present moment doesn't require their full attention. Many people use the terms "daydreaming" and "mind-wandering" interchangeably. So when you hear people say "everybody daydreams", what they mean is "everybody mind-wanders".

VIVID NARRATIVE DAYDREAMING
However, for some of us there's another kind of daydreaming. This is what I call "vivid narrative daydreaming". It's the stories we create in our imagination, the mental movies that have little or nothing to do with our real life. Throughout this book, I restrict the term "daydreaming" to mean vivid narrative daydreaming.

So what is vivid narrative daydreaming? By "vivid", I mean that you see, hear and feel every detail of the experience. If I were to ask you to imagine walking along a beach, you wouldn't have just some vague idea of a beach, you'd see all the details. You'd hear the waves breaking and the birds crying; you'd know what the weather was like and what the sun or wind felt like on your skin. All the details would just be there without you having to "decide" what to imagine.

I think of the vividness of daydreaming as being like a memory in the present tense. If I asked you to recall a conversation you had with someone yesterday, you wouldn't just remember the words as if you were reading a transcript. You'd remember where the conversation took place, the expression on the other person's face, the tone of their voice, how their words made you feel. But all those things would be images in your mind. You'd know you weren't actually reliving the conversation. Daydreaming is just the same, except you're creating the scene in your imagination right now.

By "narrative" daydreaming, I mean that the daydream has a story-like quality. There's a plot, and a cast of characters, and events unfold. It's as if we have a movie playing in our heads. We can stay in one scene for minutes or even hours at a time, and the next time we daydream, we can pick up the story where we left it. In this way, a complex plot can develop over time – it's not uncommon for daydreamers to spend years developing the details of one story.

To summarize: vivid narrative daydreaming is a style of daydreaming in which the daydreamer is living in a story of their own creation. Although it may not always be intentional to start daydreaming – we can sometimes be sucked into our other world without realizing it's happening – there is an intentional quality to it. We decide where the plot is going, we focus on it and we devote all our attention to it, blocking out the outside world for the duration of the daydream.

Although daydreaming consumes our attention, it also feels effortless. We don't have to force ourselves to concentrate on it. It's relaxing rather than tiring. When I daydream, I'm not forcing something into creation; I'm watching it unfold in my mind. I shape the broad outline of what's going to happen, but I don't consciously decide every detail.

Daydreaming is its own reward. It's about living the dream, right now, in your imagination. In its purest form, it has no purpose other than to entertain.

VIVID NARRATIVE DAYDREAMING COMES NATURALLY TO SOME PEOPLE

The ability to construct vivid narrative daydreams is an innate trait. If you have it, you were more than likely born with it, and it's something that will be with you forever. The ability doesn't go away. You can choose not to use it, but it will always be there.

The ability to daydream isn't inherently good or bad. It's part of who you are. And it's up to you to figure out how big a part you want it to play in your life and what relationship you want to have with it. And to do that, you have to understand what it is and how it can help you and harm you. This book will help you do that.

DAYDREAMING AS AN ESCAPE

Although we can choose to daydream about things that are happening in real life, many of us choose not to. Daydreaming is an escape for us, and many of us build detailed imaginary worlds. Your daydream world might look much like the world you're living in, or it might be a fantasy world filled with magical creatures. I've had a complex sci-fi fantasy going on in my head for years now, but other daydreamers might set their stories in a particular historical period or in a country they've never visited, or they might daydream about living a completely different life, perhaps as a celebrity or as someone older or younger than they are in reality. Daydreaming isn't a rehearsal for real life. It isn't a space for planning or reflecting. It's a place to explore possibilities. It's a place to wonder "what if –?" If you think of your real life as a horizontal line from the past to the present to the future, your daydreams would take you somewhere above the line. They're not tethered to your real life in any way. It's like having an extra dimension to your experience.

In the real world, our options are limited by our circumstances – the family and culture we were born into, the period of time we're living in, the educational and career opportunities open to us. But in our imagination, we don't have any of those constraints. We can explore the whole of space and time from whatever perspective we choose.

MORE THAN JUST THE STORIES IN YOUR HEAD

Often, there's more to daydreaming than just thinking. You might find you adapt your behaviour or external environment to make it easier to daydream. Daydreaming often involves some sort of repetitive physical movement. Many daydreamers pace around a room or other small space while daydreaming. Others daydream best while out for a run or walking the dog. Other daydreamers swing, bounce or rock, or fidget with a particular object such as a pen or hairbrush. Not all daydreamers need to perform repetitive movements while daydreaming, but it's common (Somer et al., 2016b).

Something else that's often intimately connected with daydreaming is music. Many daydreamers find that their daydreaming is triggered by music and/or they need to listen to music to maintain the daydream. Music sets the scene and allows you to more fully connect with the emotions the daydream evokes. It's similar to the soundtrack in a movie. Mia has been daydreaming for as long as she can remember. She uses music to drown out the real world and immerse her more fully in her daydreams. She told me: "I don't know what it is with daydreamers, but we like to listen to the music really loud. You have to turn it all the way up, so it just fills every crack, and it becomes the only thing that's around you."

THE EMOTIONS ARE REAL

Although the characters and events in our daydreams aren't real, there is one aspect of daydreaming that's very real. *Our daydreams evoke real emotions.* We can fall in love with our characters. We can be moved to tears by something that happens in the plot. Anyone who has ever cried during a movie knows that something doesn't have to be real to generate a real emotional reaction. And emotions have the power to generate chemical changes in our body. When we feel fear, our body releases adrenaline. When we feel a sense of achievement, our body releases dopamine. In this way, our thoughts can shape our reality. So although the characters and events in our daydreams aren't real, that doesn't mean our daydreams can't affect us deeply. It's normal – even inevitable – that you will become emotionally attached to your characters and your worlds.

Misconceptions about daydreaming

Let's dispel some common misconceptions. First, excessive daydreaming does not cause schizophrenia. As far as I know, there is absolutely no scientific evidence to suggest that can happen. As we'll see, daydreaming can become a destructive and debilitating addiction in its own right, but you don't need to worry about it turning into something it's not.

Second, daydreaming is fundamentally distinct from dissociative identity disorder (DID) and other forms of plurality. Our characters can become very real to us, and it's not uncommon for daydreamers to perceive their characters as having minds of their own and acting independently. But that does not make them alters or headmates, as experienced by those with DID. Our characters are people we've consciously and deliberately created; they exist in our minds at our invitation. Although we may not always consciously control what they do in the daydream, our characters can't control us outside the daydream; we know they're not real.

And third, daydreaming isn't the same as hallucinating. Our daydreams are vivid, but we know they aren't real, and we know the things we see and hear aren't actually coming in through our senses. Hallucinating is when you believe you're seeing or hearing sights or sounds that are, in reality, only in your mind. Hallucinations feel real *while you're experiencing them*. Daydreaming is vivid and detailed, but you always know it's happening in your mind and not out in the world around you. Daydreamers do not mix up fantasy and reality *while we're daydreaming*. But, depending on what you daydream about, it can get a little confusing afterwards. The quality of the daydreaming experience can be similar to a memory. And therefore, the memory of a daydream can look a lot like the memory of something that actually happened.

If your daydreams involve things that aren't real, such as having magical powers or hanging out with your favourite celebrity, then you'll always know that those events didn't happen. But if you daydream about interacting with people you know in real life, in places you visit, the context may not always be enough to remind you what was real and what wasn't. So if your daydreams tend to be realistic, you shouldn't be concerned if you occasionally wonder whether a certain event was real or a daydream. That doesn't mean you can't tell fantasy from reality.

What you daydream about

The purpose of this book is to help you have a healthy and positive relationship with your daydreaming, and I don't believe that the content of your daydreams affects that. What you choose to daydream about is your own business, and for the most part, it doesn't determine whether your daydreaming is healthy or not. However, I think it's useful to cover a few basics here, partly to introduce some of the terminology that I'll be using throughout the book, and partly to reassure you that, no matter what you daydream about, it's all normal.

YOUR DAYDREAM WORLD

I call the place where your daydreams are set your "daydream world". You may also have heard it referred to as a "paracosm". Your daydream world might be an accurate copy of somewhere you're familiar with in real life, such as your workplace or your favourite cafe. It could be somewhere you want to visit but never have, such as your ideal holiday destination. Or it might be a fictional place that's realistic or fantastical, such as a futuristic sci-fi setting or a land full of magical creatures. Anything is OK; it just depends where your imagination is happiest.

YOUR CHARACTERS

Your daydream world is usually populated with characters – the people you interact with in your daydreams. Characters can have a range of origins. They might be:

- Copies of people you know in real life
- Copies of people you know about but have never met, such as a celebrity

- A character based on a real person but with edits to their personality or backstory
- A copy of a fictional character from a book or TV show
- Someone that's entirely your own creation, not based on anyone real

Characters can stay with you for a long time. I've had some of mine for over 20 years. And that means you'll get to know them well – better than you know most real people. So don't be surprised if you get emotionally attached to them. That's normal. There's nothing weird about caring deeply for someone who doesn't exist.

However, the key thing to understand is that *your characters are not real*. That might sound obvious, but it's crucially important. Even if you base a character on someone you know in real life, even if you're daydreaming about interactions you'd like to have with that person in real life, *your character is not that person*.

As soon as you take someone real and put them in your daydreams, two things happen. First, no matter how well you know that person, you don't know how they would feel and react in every situation your daydreaming mind might put them in. So you make assumptions. And, be honest, you make your character act the way you want them to act, even if you know the real person probably wouldn't do that. In other words, you edit them. You take all the things you don't know about them, and you fill in the blanks the way you want them to be filled in. And in so doing, you create a character that's different from the person you based them on.

Second, you give them experiences the real person hasn't had. In real life, we learn and grow according to what happens to us. Daydream characters are no different. They evolve in response to the situations you put them in. Even if a character started out as a copy of someone you know, they don't stay that way for long. The real person evolves in one direction, your daydream character evolves in another. The differences between them quickly become significant.

So even when you base a character on someone you know in real life, you're still creating a fictional character. There's nothing wrong with using a real person for inspiration – *unless* you then expect the real person's life to mirror what's happening in your daydreams, or you expect the real person to act in the same way your character would. Failing to recognize that the real person will never be exactly like the character you based on them can lead to a lot of pain. Get into the habit of reminding yourself, constantly, that your characters are fictional, regardless of their origins.

YOUR DAYDREAM SELF

There is one exception to the rule that your characters aren't real. As we'll explore in Chapter 13, your daydream self can be real. Your daydream self is the person you become when you daydream. Many daydreamers daydream in first person, seeing their daydream world through the eyes of one particular character. In that case, that character is your daydream self. If you daydream in third person, you can still have a daydream self if there is one character that you particularly identify with – usually a main character who the story revolves around. But it's also possible to daydream in third person and not have a daydream self. If you daydream about a group of characters and don't feel that you're part of the story, that's perfectly OK. You're not alone in that. Mia described it to me like this: "My daydreams have nothing to do with me. It's like watching a TV series. I'm not in it. No one I know stars in it. It's just some random characters having a fantasy adventure."

If you have a daydream self, they might be an accurate representation of your real-world self, with all your flaws and imperfections. Or they might be an idealized version of you – the person you aspire to be or the person you could have been if real life hadn't got in the way. Or, if you have a fantasy daydream world, your daydream self might have supernatural powers or even be non-human. Again, there's a wide range of what we daydream about, and it's all normal.

Your daydream self is the one character that isn't necessarily fictional. When you create a character that's based on you, you aren't forced to edit them the way you are when you base a character on someone else. You really can put yourself in your daydreams. You might choose to edit yourself, to become someone different from the person you are in the real world, but that's a choice rather than a necessity. And, for that reason, your daydream self can reveal important things about who you are. We'll return to this topic in more detail in Chapter 13.

My story

When I was a child, I thought I was destined to be a novelist. Why else would I have stories bouncing around in my head all the time?

Back then, my daydreams were often inspired by the books I was reading. Around the age of ten, I was reading a lot of boarding-school stories, and so I invented my own school. It was implausibly located on a high mountain plateau, accessible by a single narrow road, isolated from the rest of the world. In my mind, I followed the adventures of a group of seven girls as they grew up, forming friendships, pursuing their own interests and learning important life lessons. I didn't put myself in my daydreams back then – I experienced my daydream world as an observer, watching the action unfold in my mind's eye – but those seven girls became my closest friends. I knew them better than I knew anyone in real life. I cheered them on when they succeeded; I felt their pain when they failed. I could spend hours at a time – and frequently did – following their adventures, pretending to live in their world.

I'd rush home from school and – if the weather was good – go straight out into the garden. And I'd bounce a ball off the back wall of the house over and over and over again. It kept my hands occupied while my mind was watching my mental movie. The adventures of my imaginary companions were more compelling than books, TV or anything in the real world.

As the years passed, the stories changed. I got into science fiction. I created a desert world – loosely based on Frank Herbert's *Dune* – which was ruled by a spirited young woman who'd inherited the throne much too young following the tragic death of her mother. When her world went to war with their much larger and more powerful neighbour, my main character had to navigate a complicated personal life while fulfilling the destiny that fate had handed to her. That world lasted for most of my teenage years, and the plot expanded to the point where, had I ever written it down, it would comfortably have made a three-volume series.

And I always assumed that one day I would write it down. Occasionally, I'd take a break from the events on my fictional planet, to daydream about my own ideal future. I'd imagine reading the glowing reviews of my first novel. I'd imagine being interviewed on TV. I'd imagine having enough celebrity status that magazines would be interested in my personal life. And, of course, that led to a fictional boyfriend and the creation of a luxury apartment with a balcony looking out over the sea.

And so it went on. Children are supposed to grow out of imaginary friends, but my characters weren't imaginary friends in that sense. I considered them my friends, but because I wasn't in most of my daydreams, I didn't interact with them. They weren't aware of my existence, just like the characters in a TV show don't know who's watching. And my stories never went away.

Throughout my life new plots sprung up. I invented new worlds. Stories took shape and grew and evolved, and then I'd replace them when a new idea captured my imagination. I've stayed with sci-fi for the most part – there have been other planets, end-of-the-world scenarios and aliens – a *lot* of aliens. And there has also been romance, and heartbreak, and complicated family scenarios, and triumph, and betrayal, and not every story has had a happy ending.

A journalist once asked me when I first realized that daydreaming like this isn't normal. And the honest answer is, I don't know. On one level, I've always known. But on another level, my daydreams are so natural, so effortless, that to me, this *is* normal. This is how I think.

For large parts of my life, my daydreaming wasn't a problem. I learned to juggle living in two worlds, because that's just how my life is. I can't imagine it any other way. But there have been times when my internal world has threatened to take over my external world. Sometimes the fantasy was so compelling that it was hard to be in reality. And sometimes devoting so much time and attention to my fictional life didn't leave enough space for the real one. And that's how it is for many daydreamers. It's not easy balancing two lives, and sometimes we don't get the balance right. But this book can help you with that.

Types of vivid narrative daydreaming

Now that we've explored what vivid narrative daydreaming consists of, let's take a closer look at the two types of vivid narrative daydreaming – immersive daydreaming and maladaptive daydreaming – and the difference between them.

Put simply, the difference between immersive daydreaming and maladaptive daydreaming lies in how your daydreaming affects you.

IMMERSIVE DAYDREAMING

If you have a good relationship with your daydreaming – if you can control when and for how long you do it, if it doesn't get in the way of you living your real life, and if you see it as an entertaining hobby – then you probably have immersive daydreaming. Immersive daydreaming is any form of vivid narrative daydreaming that isn't negatively affecting you. It isn't a mental-health problem, it isn't a disorder and it isn't anything to worry about.

MALADAPTIVE DAYDREAMING

Sometimes, however, vivid narrative daydreaming can get out of control. If you find yourself being constantly pulled into a daydream when you should be doing something else, if your daydreaming is getting in the way of your work, studying or relationships, if you feel terrible about how much time you spend lost in fantasy, or if you think there's something wrong with you because you prefer your imaginary friends to your real ones, then you might have maladaptive daydreaming disorder.

So what is "maladaptive daydreaming disorder"? We've talked about the daydreaming part, and how vivid narrative daydreaming differs from mind-wandering. But what about the maladaptive part? "Maladaptive" comes from the Latin prefix *"mal"*, meaning bad, evil or wrong, and "adaptive", which is the ability to change in response to external circumstances. So "maladaptive" means reacting in an unhealthy or harmful way to life's circumstances. Maladaptive daydreaming means using daydreaming in a way that causes problems for you.

In psychology a "disorder" is something that causes significant distress or dysfunction. We'll dig into the definition of a disorder in more detail in Chapter 2, but for now, all you need to know is that it's something that either upsets you or holds you back in some way. Whether your daydreaming causes you significant distress is something only you can decide. "Significant distress" is subjective. It can't be measured, and it's not for anyone else to tell you what you do or don't find distressing. Dysfunction is similarly difficult to measure. Whether your daydreaming prevents you from functioning adequately at work and in your social relationships can depend on what roles and responsibilities you have at this point in your life. It doesn't depend on your daydreaming alone.

WHAT MATTERS IS HOW YOUR DAYDREAMING AFFECTS YOU

Maladaptive daydreaming, by definition, has to negatively affect you. As a general rule, if your daydreaming has a neutral or positive effect on your life, then you're an immersive daydreamer. If your daydreaming negatively affects you, you're a maladaptive daydreamer.

Maladaptive daydreaming is immersive daydreaming that has taken over your life. All maladaptive daydreamers were originally immersive daydreamers, but, as we'll see in Chapter 3, not all immersive daydreamers become maladaptive daydreamers.

Maladaptive daydreaming can hinder you in a number of different ways. We'll look in more detail at the problems maladaptive daydreaming can cause in Chapter 4.

BUT WHAT IF YOU IDENTIFY WITH BOTH LABELS?

The line between immersive daydreaming and maladaptive daydreaming isn't always clear. You might be an immersive daydreamer in some situations but a maladaptive daydreamer in others. Some people can suppress their daydreaming while they're at work, and have a successful career, but find that their daydreaming interferes with maintaining real-life relationships. Some people might be able to control their daydreaming most of the time, but find that it takes over when something stressful happens. You're not necessarily one or the other. If you're a maladaptive daydreamer now, that doesn't mean you can't become an immersive daydreamer in the future and vice versa.

HOW LONG YOU SPEND DAYDREAMING

The amount of time you spend daydreaming doesn't necessarily determine whether your daydreaming is immersive or maladaptive. As a general rule, the more time you spend daydreaming, the more likely it is that your daydreaming is maladaptive. But there is no set number of hours per day beyond which your daydreaming is automatically considered maladaptive. What's manageable for one person could be seriously impairing for someone else. It very much depends on what real-life commitments you have.

Immersive daydreaming can be a legitimate hobby. Many people who have a hobby they're passionate about find ways to devote a lot of time to it without it being unhealthy. If you've found ways to fit daydreaming into your life without it being a problem, even if you're daydreaming *a lot*, it's OK. You could still be an immersive daydreamer.

The main thing to consider is how you feel about the amount of time you spend daydreaming. If you feel guilty that you can't keep your daydreaming at a more manageable level, that's a strong indicator that your daydreaming could be maladaptive. Ask yourself what *isn't* happening because of your daydreaming. Are you suffering because you're prioritizing daydreaming over more important things?

THE MOST IMPORTANT FACTOR

It's OK if you aren't sure whether your daydreaming is immersive or maladaptive. It's a continuum, and where you fall on it relative to an arbitrary line between immersive and maladaptive is a lot less important than where you fall on it relative to where you want to fall on it.

Ultimately, whether you have immersive daydreaming or maladaptive daydreaming isn't about how much you daydream or what you daydream about. It's about how you feel about your daydreaming. And that's something only you can decide.

That means that it's legitimate to diagnose yourself with maladaptive daydreaming even if you can't discuss your daydreaming with a doctor or therapist. In Chapter 6, we'll look at how and why you should talk to your doctor about your maladaptive daydreaming. I urge you to work in partnership with your doctor if that's an option for you. They can refer you for therapy, prescribe medication and help you address any coexisting problems. But, ultimately, you're the expert on what's going on in your head. If you feel that your daydreams meet the criteria for maladaptive daydreaming, it's OK to use that label.

CHAPTER 2

THE SCIENCE BEHIND MALADAPTIVE DAYDREAMING

The capacity for vivid narrative daydreaming isn't something everyone has. And it's something researchers are only just beginning to understand. For most of us, our ability to daydream in this way is an innate trait; it's simply the way we were born (Somer et al., 2016a). Our brains are wired differently from non-daydreamers. Daydreaming is how we think, how we process information, how we make sense of the world. It comes naturally to us. I've had stories in my head for as long as I can remember, and I believe they'll always be there.

Perhaps because daydreaming comes so naturally to us, or perhaps because we realize it's not natural for a lot of other people, we tend not to talk about our daydreams. And I think that's partly why scientists don't yet fully understand the causes or implications of this style of daydreaming.

Like me, Mia has been daydreaming for as long as she can remember. And, like me, she never talked about it when she was growing up. Mia told me: "I always knew that it was different. Always. I don't know how I learned that, but I know I learned that very early. I don't know if it caused me problems that early, but it definitely caused a sense of *I'm not like other people*."

"Did that make you feel you needed to hide it?" I asked her.

"Yes. I don't know if it was an active decision to hide it. It was just a passive understanding that this isn't for other people. We don't tell other people about this."

This general lack of awareness and information about vivid narrative daydreaming means that there's also a lack of awareness about maladaptive daydreaming. It's hard for non-daydreamers to understand how something as apparently harmless as daydreaming can develop into something that consumes every waking moment and makes it almost impossible to function in the real world. But, at its worst, maladaptive daydreaming can do exactly that.

In this chapter, we're going to dive into what the science tells us about maladaptive daydreaming – how common it is, how it's classified, how it's diagnosed, and, most importantly, what scientists know about treating it.

How common is maladaptive daydreaming?

Because maladaptive daydreaming is still not well known, the vast majority of maladaptive daydreamers are either undiagnosed or self-diagnosed. Therefore, it's difficult to know how many people suffer from maladaptive daydreaming.

To date, only one study (Soffer-Dudek and Theodor-Katz, 2022) has attempted to assess how many maladaptive daydreamers there are. Researchers asked different groups of people to score themselves on a questionnaire designed to detect possible maladaptive daydreaming. They then interviewed those with the highest scores to confirm whether they were maladaptive daydreamers. Their results suggested that around 2.5% of the general population experience symptoms of maladaptive daydreaming – that's one person in 40.

That figure is higher than for some relatively well-known mental-health problems, such as OCD or binge eating. So maladaptive daydreaming is more common than you might think, and is definitely something that should be more widely recognized and understood.

Unfortunately, because of the way this study was designed, the researchers were unable to draw any conclusions about immersive daydreaming. As far as I know, there are no studies looking at the frequency of immersive daydreaming. And until we know how many people are immersive daydreamers, it's impossible to say what proportion of immersive daydreamers will develop maladaptive daydreaming. That's a key question. Being an immersive daydreamer isn't something you have a choice about; it's just the way you are. But if you're an immersive daydreamer, there are things you can do to prevent your daydreaming from becoming maladaptive. And if you knew how large the risk is, you'd know how vigilant you need to be.

How is maladaptive daydreaming classified?

One of the things researchers are working to understand is how maladaptive daydreaming fits into the broader classification of problems people suffer from. This involves determining whether maladaptive daydreaming is a mental disorder in its own right or a symptom of something else. So let's look at the criteria psychologists use to classify mental-health problems and how they might apply to maladaptive daydreaming.

IS MALADAPTIVE DAYDREAMING A MENTAL DISORDER?

The *Diagnostic and Statistical Manual of Mental Disorders* (5th edn.), popularly known as the *DSM-5*, is the American Psychiatric Association's dictionary of mental-health conditions. It's what psychiatrists refer to when they diagnose someone with a mental-health problem. The *DSM-5* defines a mental disorder as:

> *a syndrome characterized by clinically significant disturbance in an individual's cognition, emotion regulation, or behavior that reflects a dysfunction in the psychological, biological, or development processes underlying mental functioning. Mental disorders are usually associated with significant distress or disability in social, occupational, or other important activities.* (American Psychiatric Association, 2022)

Let's translate that into plain English. The first sentence simply means that something in your brain isn't working properly and it's causing symptoms that have a more-than-trivial effect on how you think, feel or behave. In the context of maladaptive daydreaming – and particularly when distinguishing between maladaptive daydreaming and immersive daydreaming – the key part is the second sentence. A mental disorder usually causes significant distress or disability. Being distressed by your daydreaming doesn't mean that the daydreams themselves have to upset you. You could be distressed about not being able to control your daydreaming. And disability can be any loss of function – not being able to study because you can't focus, or not being able to make friends because you find it hard to relate to real people would both be examples of a disability caused by maladaptive daydreaming. So by the *DSM-5*'s definition, maladaptive daydreaming fits the criteria to be considered a mental disorder.

The Structured Clinical Interview for Maladaptive Daydreaming (SCIMD) is a series of questions used by researchers to establish whether someone is suffering from maladaptive daydreaming. The SCIMD specifically asks whether your daydreaming causes distress or disability: "Does your daydreaming cause significant distress or does it impair your social, academic, occupational, or other important areas of functioning?" (Somer et al., 2017b). For someone to be diagnosed with maladaptive daydreaming, they have to be able to answer yes to this question. If the answer is no, the person's daydreaming is not considered maladaptive.

But there's a problem: maladaptive daydreaming isn't currently included in the *DSM-5*. It's simply too new. Maladaptive daydreaming wasn't recognized until 2002 (Somer, 2002), and relatively little research has been done on it. There are many questions about maladaptive daydreaming that researchers don't yet know the answers to. It will take time for the diagnosis to become established enough to merit inclusion in the *DSM-5*. That means that, for now, maladaptive daydreaming isn't an "official" diagnosis, and many mental-health professionals remain unaware of it.

IS IT AN ADDICTION?
The physician, author and addiction expert, Dr Gabor Maté, defines an addictive behaviour as "any behaviour in which a person finds

temporary relief or pleasure and therefore craves, but that in the long term causes them or others negative consequences, and yet the person refuses or is unable to give it up" (2022).

There are four components in that definition. First, the behaviour has to be enjoyable or at least allow you to escape from a painful reality. Second, there has to be a strong urge to indulge in the behaviour. Third, the behaviour has to have negative long-term consequences. And fourth, it has to be something you can't just stop. Anyone who has struggled with maladaptive daydreaming for any length of time will know that it ticks all four boxes.

So maladaptive daydreaming can be both a mental disorder and an addictive behaviour. This is where we need to be crystal clear about something. At its worst, maladaptive daydreaming is not "just" daydreaming. It's not "just" indulging in idle fantasies. And it's not something you can "just" decide to stop. It's an addiction. And it's an addiction to your own thoughts – to something that's available to you at any time, regardless of what you're doing, where you are or who you're with.

Think about it this way. If you were addicted to a substance – alcohol, tobacco, drugs – you could take steps to limit your access to that substance. For example, if you wanted to stop drinking, you'd make sure there was no alcohol in your house. You'd give yourself a gap between you and the thing you're trying to stay away from. Even a relatively small gap like having to go to the store to buy alcohol gives you an opportunity to check in with yourself, to ask yourself if that's what you truly want, to question your choices.

Even with behavioural addictions, there's usually some sort of gap. Someone addicted to the internet, for example, has to pick up their phone or computer to get online. And even if that action takes only a couple of seconds, that's a couple of seconds when the more determined part of your brain can jump in and say *"Do you really want to do that?"* It's also a gap you can work with. You might decide to lock your phone away after a certain time each evening or switch off yourABi-Fi. The gap between feeling the urge and giving in to it is the space where you can fight the addiction.

With daydreaming, there's no gap. We can't physically remove ourselves from our thoughts. For many of us, daydreaming has become so automatic that we're not even conscious of feeling an urge to daydream; we just find ourselves doing it. We never have that moment when we could make a different choice.

Claire started daydreaming in childhood as a way to get the recognition and attention that her family couldn't provide. Now, as an adult, she's finding it difficult to stop daydreaming. There's no question in her mind that maladaptive daydreaming is an addiction. She told me: "I have so much sympathy for addicts, because that's what we are. We daydream just as hard as they pour themselves into their addictions, and ours is right there at our fingertips whenever we want it. And sometimes I can't run from it. Sometimes it's just all-consuming, intoxicating. I don't know how to get away from it."

Can you imagine someone addicted to alcohol staying sober if they went through life with a glass of wine permanently within arm's reach? That's what it's like trying to quit maladaptive daydreaming.

If you've been beating yourself up because you can't "just" stop daydreaming, you need to accept that there's no "just" about it. You're dealing with an addictive behaviour that's difficult to manage, and there is no shame in struggling, because the reality is that getting maladaptive daydreaming under control is hard – for anyone.

IS IT AN UNHEALTHY COPING MECHANISM?

Another way of thinking about maladaptive daydreaming is as an unhealthy coping mechanism. A coping mechanism is any strategy you use to manage difficult or painful emotions. The difference between a healthy coping mechanism and an unhealthy coping mechanism is that a healthy coping mechanism helps you to fix whatever caused the negative emotion in the first place. In contrast, an unhealthy coping mechanism numbs the pain of the negative emotion without addressing the underlying cause. It allows you to avoid or run away from the problem rather than fixing it.

Unhealthy coping mechanisms can turn into addictions. Because the unhealthy coping mechanism doesn't solve the underlying problem, the negative emotions associated with that problem don't go away; they lurk below the surface. And when you stop using your unhealthy coping mechanism, they pop right back up – which prompts you to resort to your coping mechanism again, and again, and again.

COULD IT BE BOTH?

Your maladaptive daydreaming could be both an addiction and an unhealthy coping mechanism.

Your daydreaming is an unhealthy coping mechanism if you use it to run away from uncomfortable thoughts or feelings generated by real life. In an unhealthy coping mechanism, the push is *away* from real life. Reality is not as you would like it to be, and rather than accepting that and working to change it, you run away from it by creating a better alternative in your daydreams.

However, your daydreaming is an addiction if it's so compelling that you can't give it up, despite knowing that it's messing up your life. You're so attached to your characters and your worlds that you check out of reality to spend more time with them. In other words, the pull is *toward* the daydreams.

It's a subtle distinction, and many maladaptive daydreamers will probably identify with both viewpoints. But it's important to understand the difference. If your maladaptive daydreaming is primarily an unhealthy coping mechanism, then fixing the underlying problem or learning healthier coping skills may be all that's needed. Your daydreaming might naturally subside when you no longer need to use it as an escape. But if your daydreaming has become an addiction, dealing with the underlying issue may not be enough. You'll also need to target your daydreaming directly. We'll return to all of this in more detail in Part 2.

In this section, I've painted a bleak picture of maladaptive daydreaming. If you've never thought of it as an addiction before, you might be afraid that your problem is more serious than you realized. You might be wondering whether healing is even possible. Don't worry. Healing is possible for everyone. I've done it. And, by following the strategies in this book, you can do it too.

Diagnosing and treating maladaptive daydreaming

The term "maladaptive daydreaming" was first used in 2002 (Somer, 2002), and it's only since around 2016 that researchers have begun to understand the condition and see it as distinct from other mental-health disorders. That means that many adult maladaptive daydreamers grew up thinking we were alone. We didn't have a word to describe what was going on in our heads, and so we thought we were struggling with something that was extremely rare, possibly even unique to us. But, as we've seen, maladaptive daydreaming isn't that unusual. Worldwide there are millions of us.

WE ARE NO LONGER ISOLATED

In the last few decades, the internet and social media have become part of our daily lives. That's been huge for maladaptive daydreamers. For one thing, the world is more connected than ever before, so no matter how unusual our experience is, we can find people who understand. But, just as importantly, we're now connected to an unimaginably huge encyclopaedia through our phones. And there are no filters. Anyone can post online about their experience and it's out there for other people to find and relate to. When I was young, I had to go to the library to research things that caught my interest. And the information I could find was restricted to what someone "authoritative" felt was worth publishing. Even if there had been a word for maladaptive daydreaming when I was growing up, I'd have been limited in what I could find out about it. But now there's a wealth of information available to me from the privacy of my own phone. Maladaptive daydreamers can research their condition and connect with each other in a way that's never been possible before.

Like me, Mia started maladaptively daydreaming before the condition had a name. She'd made several unsuccessful attempts to find out why her mind worked so differently from other people's. But then one day she came across an unfamiliar word that led her to discover that she was a maladaptive daydreamer.

Mia recalled: "It was in college. I remember I was in the stacks of my library, and I was reading a book about the Brontës, which had nothing to do with the paper I was researching. It talked about the Brontë sisters' paracosm called Glass Town. And that word 'paracosm' stuck out to me. I thought, *"is this what I have?"* So I googled 'paracosm' plus other words – 'world inside my head', just descriptors of what a paracosm might be. Eventually maladaptive daydreaming popped up."

These days, it's much easier for maladaptive daydreamers to find the name of their condition. And, in general, that's a good thing. But it does carry some risks. Most of what you'll find online about maladaptive daydreaming is not authoritative. A lot of it is useful, but some of it is just plain wrong. Please get into the habit of questioning everything you read and weighing up whether it fits your experience and whether it's consistent with other things you've read.

HOW TO GET A DIAGNOSIS

Before maladaptive daydreaming becomes an official diagnosis that's generally understood and accepted by mental-health professionals, there needs to be a set of universally recognized diagnostic criteria. The website of the International Consortium for Maladaptive Daydreaming Research (ICMDR) has a useful tool called the 16-item Maladaptive Daydreaming Scale (MDS-16). The MDS-16 is a questionnaire that can be used to assess whether someone is likely to be a maladaptive daydreamer. The MDS-16 is *not* intended to be used as a diagnostic tool – it cannot definitively tell you whether or not your daydreaming is maladaptive, but it does give you a rough idea. However, the MDS-16 is primarily intended to distinguish maladaptive daydreaming from mind-wandering. Immersive daydreamers, who have vivid narrative daydreams but aren't negatively affected by them, will likely have intermediate scores on the MDS-16. It's also important to note that what you score on the MDS-16 will probably fluctuate in the short and long term as your relationship with your daydreaming changes.

The MDS-16 should be followed up by the SCIMD, which should be conducted by a qualified mental-health professional. It is the

SCIMD that comes closest to providing a diagnosis of maladaptive daydreaming. The SCIMD is freely available on the ICMDR website, so it's possible to have a go at assessing yourself with it, but please be aware that the results are likely to be less accurate if you try to do the assessment without the support of your doctor.

Diagnosing maladaptive daydreaming isn't an exact science. The diagnostic criteria aren't yet universally agreed, many mental-health professionals are still unaware of the condition, and there isn't a quick test you can take that will give you a definitive yes-or-no answer.

ARE THERE ANY SCIENTIFICALLY VALIDATED TREATMENTS?

Even though maladaptive daydreaming isn't in the *DSM-5*, there are a number of research groups across the world working to understand it and figure out how to treat it. Prominent among these is Professor Eli Somer's group at the University of Haifa. One of Somer's students, Oren Herscu, conducted a study in which maladaptive daydreamers were treated using a self-guided web-based programme (Herscu et al., 2023).

At the time of writing, Herscu et al.'s study is the *only* randomized controlled trial of a treatment for maladaptive daydreaming to have been published in the research literature. Their results were impressive, however, with one in four study participants overcoming their maladaptive daydreaming by the end of the eight-week programme and the majority of them remaining well six months later.

The exact treatment programme that Herscu et al. used is the subject of further research and is not yet freely available. But the key parts of the programme are education, motivation enhancement, mindfulness and self-monitoring. We'll cover all of those in this book.

The exciting thing about Herscu et al.'s treatment programme is that it's internet-based self-help. The study participants didn't have one-to-one time with a therapist. And that proves that maladaptive daydreamers *can* recover without therapy, which is great news if you're reading this book because therapy isn't an option for you.

WHERE TO GET RELIABLE INFORMATION

As I mentioned above, there's a lot of misinformation about maladaptive daydreaming circulating online, so you need to be careful about what you read. At the end of this book, I've compiled a brief list of websites that I believe give helpful and reliable information about maladaptive daydreaming. There are two in particular that I highly recommend. The first is the website of the ICMDR, where you can download and read the studies I've referenced in this chapter. And the second is the website of the International Society for Maladaptive Daydreaming (ISMD), which is run by a team of psychologists and people with lived experience of maladaptive daydreaming.

CHAPTER 3

WHY DID YOUR DAYDREAMING BECOME MALADAPTIVE?

Before we get into why your daydreaming became maladaptive, I need you to understand that *it was not your fault*. You didn't do anything wrong. Your maladaptive daydreaming is a response to circumstances that were, in all probability, outside your control. You don't need to blame yourself for this. But you do need to understand why it happened.

One of the things about being an immersive daydreamer is that you can disconnect from reality whenever you want to. There's nothing wrong with disconnecting so that you can enjoy your daydream world when reality doesn't need you. The problems start when you disconnect from reality because reality isn't a nice place to be.

Daydreaming is your mind trying to keep you safe

When our subconscious perceives a threat, it triggers the fight-or-flight response. But sometimes, physically fighting the threat or physically fleeing the threatening situation are both impossible. Daydreaming gives us another option: we can flee mentally. We can remove ourselves from the stressful, scary or painful situation by creating a daydream where we control everything and the threat doesn't exist.

We typically learn at a young age that we can flee stressful situations by dropping into a daydream. Daydreaming makes us feel better, at least temporarily. We can make the bad stuff go away by imagining a world where it didn't happen.

Using daydreaming occasionally to self-soothe isn't a problem. But it's easy to go from there to relying on daydreaming as a way to cope with difficult emotions. Unfortunately, it's not uncommon for this to happen in childhood. It just depends on when life first throws more at you than you can handle.

DAYDREAMING AS A CHILDHOOD TRAUMA RESPONSE

As young children, we often don't have the skills or autonomy necessary to solve our problems. Fighting back or fleeing by changing our circumstances probably aren't realistic. So our minds do what they have to do to keep us safe. They disconnect us from reality.

The effects of early-life trauma can last well into adult life and set the stage for a range of mental-health problems. But it isn't just the big scary things – physical or sexual abuse, the death of a parent, witnessing something horrific – that count as trauma. One way to think about trauma is as *any experience that threatened to cause you more pain and suffering than you could handle at the time*. What you could handle at the time depended on a lot of things – how old you were, what sort of person you are, what else was going on in your life. Something that one child can shrug off might be traumatic for another child.

Also, trauma isn't always about bad things that happened to you. It can be about good things that didn't happen. You might not have consciously realized you felt lonely, unloved or invalidated, but your subconscious mind recognized that something wasn't right and created a daydream world to meet a need that wasn't being met in real life.

So maladaptive daydreaming can start in childhood. But if you remember daydreaming when you were very young, that doesn't necessarily mean you had maladaptive daydreaming. You could have been indulging in healthy immersive daydreaming.

We have fewer responsibilities in childhood. We don't have to earn an income or organize a household. There are fewer demands on our time. And, therefore, it's possible for children to daydream for several hours a day without it being a problem. For children, the key difference between immersive daydreaming and maladaptive daydreaming lies in what the daydreaming is doing for them. Choosing to daydream because it's fun, treating it as a form of play, is fine. But if a child *needs* to daydream to escape reality, that's a warning sign that all is not well in that child's life.

WAS YOUR CHILDHOOD DAYDREAMING MALADAPTIVE?

To work out whether your daydreaming was maladaptive when you were a child, try to remember what it meant to you. Did you need to go to your daydream world to avoid something or someone? Or were your daydream friends the only friends you had? If so, then your daydreaming could well have been maladaptive. Maladaptive daydreaming can develop at any age; all it needs is for real life to be something you want to escape from.

What was going on in your life when your daydreaming first became maladaptive? How might those events have shaped your beliefs about yourself and the world? Did you receive messages that you weren't good enough or that you'd be loved only if you behaved in a certain way? Or did people say hurtful things about your daydreaming, telling you that you were too old to have imaginary friends or that talking to yourself was the first sign of madness? Those messages might have stuck in your mind and become limiting beliefs that are still holding you back many years later. If that's the case, and awareness of where those beliefs came from isn't enough to shift them, then you might need to talk to a qualified therapist. We will come back to how therapy can be helpful for maladaptive daydreamers in Chapter 8.

Claire's story

Claire's childhood was shaped by the needs of her disabled father. Her daydreams became her refuge, the place where she could find companionship, feel her emotions and receive the attention she wasn't getting anywhere else.

"My daydreams are my attempt at comfort. I had a dad who was disabled and in a lot of pain, so he was not always himself. He would have these wild mood swings, where he would be fine and happy one minute and then angry or critical the next. And so a lot of attention was placed on him, because he couldn't do a lot for himself. From a young age, I helped to take care of him.

"I never learned how to deal with emotions. They were pretty much frowned upon. It was like, be happy and just get over it. And I've always been really sensitive, so I needed a lot of emotional support that I just didn't get.

"I have a lot of imaginary friends, and I have this whole other world that I go to. It kind of crosses over into my real life in places, and in other places it doesn't. I'm famous and I'm rich and everybody loves me. And I have this big house, and I let all of my friends come and go as they please. So I constantly have all of these people around me, building me up and supporting me and trying to help me get through all of these problems that I have in real life. In my daydreams, I have people who try to help me get better, and for a long time that was my therapy.

"I started seeing a real therapist in March of this year for the first time in my life. When I started going to therapy, I didn't understand how much my childhood had hurt me. I thought it was not normal, but not as bad as it turned out that it was when I started telling my therapist some of the experiences I had when I was a kid. I was pretty severely neglected. I think my parents loved me; it was just they had a lot of hurt from when they were kids, and they didn't have the awareness to try to fix things. They probably didn't even realize there was a problem. I've started to realize I daydream because I want connection that I'm not getting."

In childhood, Claire turned to daydreaming to meet needs that were not being met in the real world. But because daydreaming was the only coping mechanism she knew, it became the thing she turned to every time life wasn't giving her what she needed. And over time, she became dependent on it. That's how daydreaming typically becomes maladaptive.

Maladaptive daydreaming can start at any age

Although maladaptive daydreaming is often the result of childhood trauma, it doesn't have to be. If your childhood met all of your emotional needs, you might not have discovered your talent for daydreaming until you were older. But your ability to immersively daydream was always there. At some point, you were bound to discover it. And once you discovered what a loving, safe and compelling world you could create in your imagination, it was always going to be tempting to take yourself there when real life got difficult.

That's why it's possible to develop maladaptive daydreaming for the first time as a teenager or an adult. The potential for your daydreaming to become maladaptive never goes away. Even if you've overcome maladaptive daydreaming in the past, there will always be a risk of it coming back. The only way to avoid it is to learn healthier ways of dealing with life's challenges.

HOW DAYDREAMING MIGHT CHANGE WITH AGE

Your relationship with your daydreaming might change as you make the transition from childhood to adulthood. As you get older, you tend to have more choices *and* more responsibilities. When you are a child, your caregivers make many of your decisions for you, but as you get older, you have more options about how you spend your time and who you spend it with. You have to take responsibility for making the choices that will be best for you in the long term.

As an adult, you'll have to earn a living while also maintaining a home, running errands and perhaps caring for children or other family members. Being an adult comes with responsibilities that aren't always much fun. So you might be tempted to avoid those responsibilities by daydreaming.

As your life circumstances change, the amount of free time you have will also change. That could move your daydreaming from immersive to maladaptive without the daydreaming itself changing. As a university student, I could daydream for two or three hours a day without it being too much of a problem. But 15 years later, when I was a new mum to two tiny babies, I barely had time to take a shower. Daydreaming two or three hours a day at that point would have caused major problems. Thankfully, my daydreaming faded into the background for a few years when my children were little.

YOU CAN HEAL AND RELAPSE AT ANY TIME

As we'll see in Chapter 6, the best way to overcome maladaptive daydreaming is to turn it back into immersive daydreaming. That means you'll have control over it and be able to make it work for you rather than against you. In most cases, I don't think it's necessary or helpful to stop daydreaming completely. But if you can control your daydreaming, you have a choice. You can choose not to daydream, and for some people that may be the right thing to do. But that doesn't mean you're no longer a daydreamer; it just means you're a daydreamer who chooses not to daydream. There's a difference.

That difference is important because being a daydreamer means you have to remain vigilant – always – against the possibility of your daydreaming getting out of control. Daydreaming feels good, and it's only ever a thought away. That combination makes it a compelling coping mechanism. Even if you've overcome maladaptive daydreaming in the past, the possibility of falling back into it never goes away. The way to avoid relapsing is to learn healthier coping skills – a topic we'll return to in Chapter 9.

DAYDREAMING AS AN ADULT

Our society views daydreaming differently in children and adults, and this can affect how you feel about your daydreaming. In childhood, daydreaming is seen as imaginative play. It's accepted, and in an era when people worry about children spending too much time on screens, it may even be encouraged. But as an adult, being a daydreamer is associated with being lazy or distracted. It's seen as a barrier to productivity and a way of evading responsibility. It doesn't have to be any of those things, but if you hear that message often enough, it's hard not to believe it. Too often, daydreaming is seen as a childhood activity that we're supposed to grow out of, which can be shame-inducing if you're still daydreaming in your 20s or 30s and you realize you can't stop.

But daydreaming isn't something you just grow out of. The ability to immersively daydream never goes away. And if your daydreaming has become maladaptive, it isn't going to flip back to immersive on its own. You need to make the decision to change. But the good news is that it's a choice you can make. As an adult, escaping from your problems by daydreaming isn't the only option, the way it might have been when you were a child. It might feel like the only option if you never learned healthier coping strategies. But it's never too late to learn how to handle things differently.

Sola's story

Sola Lee is a life coach who's using her experiences as a maladaptive daydreamer to help others overcome the condition. I asked her to tell me about her childhood and her earliest memories of daydreaming.

"I don't ever remember not being a daydreamer. I was the kind of child who believed in fairy tales or mystical things, because those were in my daydreams. They were real. And this was just my way of thinking. I didn't know it was particularly different from anyone else. I was always staring out the window, always looking at the sky. At the age of five or six, I was more interested in my daydreams than in hanging out with my friends."

"And back then, did you think it was a problem?" I asked her.

"That wasn't even a question. It was just the way I was. I was born that way. I didn't find it uncomfortable or anything."

"When did you start to see it as a problem?"

"I lived abroad for about four years. And then, when I was 15, I came back to Korea for high school. And the pressure to fit in was real, and it was huge. And that was when I thought, not just the maladaptive daydreaming but the unique person I am, was something that I needed to repress. And I started artificially repressing myself because how I saw myself didn't align with the societal norm to be academic, to be focussed. What I didn't know then was that I was creating a whole different world in my head that contrasted with the reality I was struggling with. It was years later when I sought therapy that I learned how my daydreams were interfering with my reality. It took me two years to fully process this as a problem I wanted to solve."

"Do you remember when you first heard the term 'maladaptive daydreaming'?"

"I think it was during my second year of college. That was when my reality was just falling down. I started searching for terms like 'overthinking' or 'anxiety issues'. And that's how I came across maladaptive daydreaming. I think I was more relieved than anything, because I was trying to identify myself. I was wondering if I had ADHD. But maladaptive daydreaming was a more exact explanation of who I was. And honestly, I loved it. I loved having an explanation.

"I remember reading one post in BuzzFeed. It was written by someone who identified herself as a maladaptive daydreamer. And that was super helpful, to read about a person going through similar events to what I have gone through. When you're going through some struggle, just the fact that another person is also going through that gives you a sense of relief."

Sola's story is typical. She remembers preferring daydreaming to playing with other children when she was a young child, but because daydreaming came so naturally to her, she never questioned it or saw it as a problem. It was only as she got older that she realized she was different from other people, and with that awareness came a belief that she had to hide her difference in order to fit in. And because she never talked about her daydreaming, it was years before she discovered that other people daydream in the same way. The sense of relief that Sola felt when she found she wasn't alone is something many immersive and maladaptive daydreamers feel when they realize that their condition has a name.

An escape not a solution

Maladaptive daydreaming nearly always begins as a protective response to something that isn't as it should be – it's either an escape from something bad that's happening or an attempt to compensate for something good that isn't happening. Something is wrong, and your mind tries to put it right in perhaps the only way that's available to you at the time. In the beginning, maladaptive daydreaming isn't a problem, it's an attempt to solve a problem.

But although daydreaming can provide an escape, it can't fix the underlying problem. And when we use daydreaming as the *only* way we deal with our problems, that's when it gets out of control. Daydreaming is always going to be an attractive response to real-life pain. It feels good. It numbs the pain temporarily. But when we stop daydreaming, the pain comes right back.

The damaging thing is that every time we escape from our pain by daydreaming, we miss an opportunity to deal with that pain in a healthier way: a way that helps solve the problem instead of just running away from it. Many maladaptive daydreamers started using their daydreaming to escape from pain when they were too young to have many other options. But when maladaptive daydreaming persists over many years, we don't learn healthier coping strategies. And that makes us dependent on the unhealthy coping strategy of daydreaming. But when daydreaming starts causing problems of its own that we want to escape from, we find ourselves in a vicious downward spiral that's hard to break out of.

Once we get used to using daydreaming to escape negative emotions, we tend to use it to avoid *all* negative emotions. So even if the situation you were using your daydreaming to escape from resolves over time, you're left with the belief that the only way to respond to painful thoughts and feelings is to run away from them by daydreaming.

Negative emotions are a part of life. No one can avoid them completely. So although you should try to limit the stress in your life as much as possible, you'll also need to find healthier ways of coping with your problems. We'll come back to this in Chapters 8 and 9.

For now, what I want you to understand is that your daydreaming became maladaptive when something happened to you that was more than you could cope with. That thing wasn't your fault. And your mind did the most helpful thing it could. It protected you by giving you somewhere safer and more comforting to be. At the time, that might have been the best option available.

You don't daydream because you aren't good enough; you daydream because real life wasn't good enough for you. So please don't blame yourself for having maladaptive daydreaming. It doesn't make you a failure. It doesn't make you wrong or broken. It's simply a coping mechanism that got out of hand, and now it's time to take back control. And that's OK because in Part 2 of this book I'm going to show you exactly how to do that.

Are there any taboo daydream topics?

Daydreamers often wonder whether it's OK to daydream about certain topics. For example, should you be concerned if you daydream about being hurt or about hurting someone else? What if your daydream self's race, gender identity or sexual orientation doesn't match yours? Is it creepy to imagine deeply personal interactions with someone you barely know in real life? All of these questions are common.

My belief is that your imagination is a safe space where nothing is off limits. You don't need to worry about, or censor, what happens in your daydreams provided that two conditions are met: first, you know it's just fantasy and second, you don't let your fantasy spill over into real life. If it's just an idea that you're playing with in your head, and it stays in your head, you don't need to be concerned. Much of what we daydream about is meaningful on some level, and you can probably learn a lot about yourself if you get curious about your daydream themes. However, our daydreams tend to speak to us in metaphors rather than literally.

As you get more in touch with your daydreaming, you might figure out why certain themes come up. But if you don't, don't worry about it. You might just be following what feels like an interesting plot.

WHAT IF YOUR DAYDREAMS ARE UPSETTING?

It's not unusual to daydream about things that upset you. As we've seen, just because the people and events in your daydreams aren't real doesn't mean the emotions aren't real. They are. It's not weird or unhealthy if your daydreams make you cry sometimes or if you have feelings for someone who doesn't exist. That's a normal part of what it means to be a daydreamer.

But what if the same distressing themes turn up in your daydreams over and over again? What if you imagine horrible things happening to you or you make your characters suffer? Why does that happen when daydreaming is supposed to be fun?

A study into the fantasies of maladaptive daydreamers (Somer et al., 2021) found that upsetting themes are common. Almost 60% of maladaptive daydreamers daydream about death, and over 50% daydream about revenge or physical violence. And it's more common to daydream about being the victim of violence than the perpetrator of it. But this study was conducted specifically on maladaptive daydreamers, so it's not known whether immersive daydreamers are less likely to create upsetting plots.

One reason you might daydream about dark or upsetting things is that it gives you an opportunity to process negative emotions that are spilling over from real life. This could be in relation to something difficult that's already happened, or it could be your way of dealing with anxiety about something you fear might happen. The way it shows up in your daydreams is often metaphorical. You might not daydream about exactly the thing you're worried about, but you might play out similar ideas and emotions. Your daydreams are your mind's way of reassuring you that even if the worst did happen, you'd be able to survive it.

Another reason you might daydream about something horrible happening to you or to someone close to you is because those moments of crisis are often followed by moments when people no longer take each other for granted. Maybe your character needs to have a near-death experience so that another character will realize they can't live without them. Sometimes what you long for is the caring, loving and honest conversation that follows that moment of crisis.

A final reason you might daydream about upsetting things is so that it can all come right in the end. In all the best novels, the main character suffers at some point, and watching them transcend that suffering and find happiness or fulfilment is part of what makes a great story. Your daydreams are no different. If nothing bad ever happened, you wouldn't have a plot. You might not need to look for a deeper meaning behind the negative daydreams; you might just be crafting a great story.

Don't be concerned if your daydreams have dark or upsetting themes. It's common and there are many possible reasons for it. As you work through this book, you'll probably start to understand why you daydream about the things you do.

Maladaptive daydreaming can't be viewed in isolation

In this chapter, we've learned that maladaptive daydreaming begins as your mind's attempt to solve a problem. And that's why you can't overcome maladaptive daydreaming in isolation. You have to see your daydreaming in the context of the rest of your life. In Part 2, we'll look at how overcoming shame, fixing your problems and working on your real life all make it easier to manage your daydreaming. But before we dive into that, you need to understand why it's worth putting so much time and effort into overcoming your maladaptive daydreaming. In the next chapter, we'll look at all the ways in which your maladaptive daydreaming is harming you.

Worksheet: Is your daydreaming immersive or maladaptive?

The worksheet that accompanies this chapter will help you to understand whether your daydreaming is immersive or maladaptive. It will also help you start thinking about what needs to change for you to have a healthier relationship with your daydreaming.

Download the worksheet at:
https://daydreamplace.com/extreme-imagination/worksheet-chapter3.pdf

CHAPTER 4

HOW CAN MALADAPTIVE DAYDREAMING HARM YOU?

Now that you understand what maladaptive daydreaming is and why you might have developed it, let's look at the ways maladaptive daydreaming can affect you, why maladaptive daydreaming is a problem and why it's worth your time and effort to get it under control.

Maladaptive daydreaming can impact almost every aspect of your life. It affects how you see the world, how you relate to other people and how you show up at work and with your family and friends. And it can influence how you see yourself. Maladaptive daydreamers tend to be highly self-critical.

Before we start looking at how to overcome your maladaptive daydreaming, you need to understand that recovery isn't easy. If it was, you'd never have got trapped in your daydreams in the first place. Overcoming maladaptive daydreaming will take time and effort. You'll need to stay motivated long enough to see results. And the way you do that is by understanding just how much harm your maladaptive daydreaming is causing you and how many areas of your life it's affecting.

In this chapter, we're going to look at all the ways in which your maladaptive daydreaming might be harming you.

You waste a lot of time

Daydreaming takes time. Maladaptive daydreaming takes a lot of time. It's not uncommon for maladaptive daydreamers to spend four to six hours a day, or more, lost in their fantasy worlds. And that time has to come from somewhere. We all have 24 hours in each day. If you're spending six of them in your daydream world, that's six hours you aren't spending in the real world – time when you aren't studying, or hanging out with your friends, or pursuing your goals.

Chet told me just how extreme his daydreaming can become: "Sometimes I would just daydream for 20 to 40 hours in a row, playing out entire days in the lives of characters. Most of the daydream would be the characters, plot, their emotions, their cathartic epiphanies and plot climaxes, etc."

When your maladaptive daydreaming has been consuming big chunks of your time for months, or even years, you'll notice the effect. You'll notice the things you're not getting done. And, just as importantly, you'll notice the things other people *are* getting done. You'll see your friends progressing in their careers, meeting people, living their lives. And your life is on hold. You're in much the same place you were this time last year, and the year before. You feel as though you're missing out on life.

Mia's daydreaming got so out of control when she was a teenager that her parents thought she might be anaemic. But even when they took her to a doctor, she couldn't tell either her parents or the doctor that she was daydreaming. She explained: "Coming into the teenage years was really where it started to shine through that I wasn't just a weird kid. Something's wrong. This isn't normal, and it's so not normal that now other people can see it too. I don't pace when I daydream. So I would lie in bed and pretend to be sleeping. I'd come home from school, I'd go upstairs, go to bed, and I would not get out of my bed until school the next day. And on weekends I just didn't leave my bedroom. And on vacations I just didn't leave my bedroom. So much so that my parents thought I was anaemic, because why else would somebody sleep that much?"

You don't know how to handle romantic relationships

Maladaptive daydreamers can struggle with romantic relationships. For many of us, romance is a major theme in our daydream world. And that can lead to problems in real life.

Romantic relationships can follow a predictable pattern. You meet someone you like. You go on a first date with them. Everything is great. And then you put that person into your daydreams. But you don't know them that well yet. So you have to make assumptions about who they are – what they like and don't like, how they would react in a given situation, even things about their background that you don't yet know. In other words, you create a daydream character, and you make that character exactly what you want them to be.

In these daydreams, you're building the relationship. You start to love and trust this person. Daydreamers can fall in love quickly because we can spend so much time with someone in our imagination.

In the real world, this is someone you've only just met. In your imagination, this is your soulmate who you've spent a whole lifetime with. That's a big disconnect. And if you're not careful, you start expecting the real person to live up to the expectations you have of the character you based on them. And when they don't, you've messed up the relationship before you ever gave it a chance.

You don't have many friends

Friendships can be hard for daydreamers. The culprit is often our distractibility. It's hard for us to stay present when we're with our friends, and we don't think about them when we're not with them. It doesn't occur to us to pick up the phone and call them, because we're hanging out with our daydream characters. But to our friends, this can come across as disinterest or a lack of caring.

Another reason we struggle with friendships is that many maladaptive daydreamers don't have great social skills. As we saw in Chapter 3, maladaptive daydreaming often starts in childhood. When our peers were learning to navigate the give-and-take of real friendships, we were pacing around our rooms talking to our characters. And you can't learn social skills from your characters. Your characters never fall out with you, so they can't teach you how to deal with rejection or how to repair a friendship after a misunderstanding. You never have to compromise, because your characters always want what you want. You don't learn to forgive, because your characters never do anything you need to forgive them for.

If you didn't learn how to make friends in childhood, it's hard to figure it out when you become an adult.

You don't set or achieve goals

Maladaptive daydreamers find it hard to set and achieve goals. In our daydreams, we can be, do or have anything we want, instantly. It doesn't take any time or effort.

In real life, you have to work for what you want. It can be hard, it can mean you have to sacrifice other things that are less important to you, and there will be times when you don't feel like doing the work. For non-daydreamers, visualizing the end result can motivate them to keep going when the work gets hard. But for daydreamers, it can have the opposite effect. When we visualize the end result, it can feel so real that we wonder if it's worth making the effort to have it in reality, when we can have it right now in our imagination. So we tend to daydream about it instead of working toward it.

When there's a huge gap between where you are now and where you want to be, you don't see it as the challenge it is. You don't see an opportunity for learning or personal growth; you see an unbridgeable chasm. You never learned that you can set a goal and work toward it. Your daydreaming taught you that if real life isn't giving you what you want, you should just imagine it instead.

You lose your sense of self

It took me decades to understand the effect my daydreaming had on my sense of who I am. There was a disconnect between the person I was in real life and the person I was in my daydreams. I believed that because my daydreams weren't real, my daydream self wasn't real either. And because the physical world around me is real, I thought the person I am in the real world must be the real me. But in my head, I was spending a lot of time being someone else. And I was happy as that someone else. I never felt entirely comfortable being real-world me.

When we have that disconnect between who we are in our daydreams and who we are in the real world, we don't know which version is real. And when you aren't sure who you are, you try to be what other people want you to be. You let other people's ideas of what you "should" do with your life dictate the path you follow. But if that path isn't right for you, you'll feel it. You'll know, deep down, that you're living a life that wasn't meant for you. And if you don't recognize that feeling for what it is, it can lead to a lot of confusion and depression.

Some daydreamers get frustrated when they can't show up as their confident, awesome daydream self in the real world. That frustration can lead to judgement and negative self-talk. But remember, it's easy to be confident in your imagination, where you control the outcome and there's no possibility of failure. It's a lot harder in real life, when you don't know how other people will react and you can't press the rewind button if it all goes wrong.

You don't mind-wander

In Chapter 1, we looked at the difference between daydreaming and mind-wandering. Mind-wandering is what non-daydreamers do when the outside world doesn't require their full attention. One study suggested that non-daydreamers mind-wander about 50% of the time (Killingsworth and Gilbert, 2010). Daydreamers spend most of that time daydreaming. Daydreaming is more fun than simply letting your thoughts drift from topic to topic, but mind-wandering serves a purpose. It's how we make random connections and get flashes of insight. How often do you hear about someone having a lightbulb moment while in the shower or walking the dog? By daydreaming instead of mind-wandering, we're cutting ourselves off from those insights.

Daydreaming also uses more mental energy than mind-wandering. When we mind-wander, we don't put any effort into controlling what we're thinking about. But when we daydream, we're directing the plot and focussing on how we want the story to unfold. We might even back up a scene and re-run it if it didn't go quite right. That uses mental energy, and if you're daydreaming instead of mind-wandering for 50% of your day, it can be exhausting.

Our daydreams evoke real emotions. That's part of what makes them so compelling. But we're not designed to be in a state of high emotion all the time. If your daydreams tend to be an emotional rollercoaster, you might never feel truly relaxed, and that isn't good for your mental or physical health.

You run away from challenging emotions

Negative emotions are a part of life. We feel them for a reason. They're a signal that something is wrong and needs addressing. But they're also uncomfortable. We tend to escape from that discomfort by daydreaming. But when we avoid our negative emotions, we don't give ourselves an opportunity to listen to their message and resolve the underlying issue.

When we're focussed on our daydream world, we're not paying attention to the sensations in our bodies. Negative emotions are usually accompanied by physical sensations – perhaps a tightness in the chest when we're anxious, or our face getting hot when we're angry – but as daydreamers, we unconsciously train ourselves to ignore those sensations. That makes it harder to get in touch with our negative emotions.

You keep making the same mistakes

Like negative emotions, mistakes are a part of life. In fact, you can often make more progress by learning from your mistakes than by celebrating your successes. But learning from your mistakes means you have to reflect on those mistakes. You have to consider what went wrong and what you could do differently next time. Most of us would rather daydream than critically examine a real-life situation that went wrong. And that reluctance to face the real world means we don't give ourselves the chance to learn and grow.

You stay in your comfort zone

The American author Neale Donald Walsch famously said "life begins at the end of your comfort zone". When we stay in our comfort zone and avoid challenging ourselves, we don't learn what we're truly capable of. We don't grow into someone better than we are now. And we miss out on potentially exciting and meaningful experiences. Daydreaming can't push you out of your comfort zone, because you control the outcome. It doesn't matter what wild adventures your daydream self gets up to, there's no actual challenge, there's no risk of failure, there's no uncertainty. So there's no personal growth in your daydream world, no matter what you do there.

You judge yourself for being a daydreamer

This can be a key issue for a lot of maladaptive daydreamers. If you feel deep-rooted shame or distress about your daydreaming, even if, objectively, your daydreaming isn't causing you too many problems, you're still suffering. And if your daydreaming is causing you to suffer, then it's maladaptive.

But the shame isn't coming from the daydreaming itself or the consequences of it; it's coming from your beliefs about your daydreaming. Those beliefs often form young, usually as a result of messages you picked up from other people.

As a child, one phrase I heard a lot was "talking to yourself is the first sign of madness". That wasn't compatible with a belief that having conversations with my characters was normal or acceptable. You might have been ridiculed for having imaginary friends, people might have said you looked weird when you were pacing, or you might have been laughed at for wanting to be a singer, celebrity, superhero or whatever it is you become in your daydreams. Whatever happened, somehow you got the idea that daydreaming isn't OK or that it isn't something "normal" people do. But at the same time, you knew, deep down, that it's part of who you are. And when you start to believe that who you are is not OK, that's what creates shame.

If you believe that it's not OK to daydream, regardless of where that belief came from, then even moderate daydreaming will be a problem for you because it will stop you from liking yourself. In this case, it's not how your daydreaming affects you that's the problem, it's your attitude to your daydreaming.

We'll look at shame in more detail in Chapter 7, but I want you to know that almost all maladaptive daydreamers feel shame. It's important to acknowledge that, because the shame you feel about being a daydreamer will be one of the biggest barriers to overcoming your maladaptive daydreaming.

Worksheet: How is maladaptive daydreaming affecting you?

The worksheet that accompanies this chapter will help you understand which areas of your life are being affected by your maladaptive daydreaming. You'll come up with a score that represents the impact your maladaptive daydreaming is having on you, and that will give you a benchmark against which to measure your progress as you work through this book.

Download the worksheet at:
https://daydreamplace.com/extreme-imagination/worksheet-chapter4.pdf

CHAPTER 5

OTHER CONDITIONS THAT ARE ASSOCIATED WITH MALADAPTIVE DAYDREAMING

Maladaptive daydreaming rarely, if ever, exists in isolation. In one study (Somer et al., 2017a), researchers looked at what other conditions are associated with maladaptive daydreaming. Every single maladaptive daydreamer in their (admittedly small) study group had at least one additional diagnosis. Over 95% of them had more than one. Three-quarters of the maladaptive daydreamers in the study met the diagnostic criteria for ADHD, 71% had anxiety and two-thirds had depression. But the most frightening finding of all was that over a quarter had attempted suicide. Maladaptive daydreaming clearly cannot be dismissed as a fictitious or trivial problem.

Why do so many maladaptive daydreamers have poor mental health?

In Chapter 4, we looked at the ways maladaptive daydreaming can harm you. If you don't have a satisfying life – if you're falling behind in your career and you're socially isolated – it's easy to see why you might develop depression. And if you can't tolerate negative emotions and don't have healthy coping strategies, you'll be prone to anxiety. So it's logical that maladaptive daydreaming might cause other mental-health problems.

Alternatively, being an immersive daydreamer and having poor mental health could increase the likelihood that your immersive daydreaming will become maladaptive. By definition, mental-health problems are distressing, and if the only way you can escape from that distress is by daydreaming, you'll become dependent on daydreaming as a coping mechanism.

Alice, who we'll meet again in Chapter 15, has recently been diagnosed with borderline personality disorder. Her daydreaming is part of how she manages it. She says: "Currently I really need my characters. My mental health has got so bad, and maladaptive daydreaming is my relief from that. I don't know what I would do without my characters and without my daydreams. I think it's really brilliant that our minds have created this coping mechanism for those of us who don't have another way to cope. There are a lot of other ways that are more unhealthy or potentially life-threatening that people use to cope, but for me it's always been my daydreams. I am in a place right now where I really deeply appreciate that about my brain."

In Alice's case, it's clear that her mental-health problems are feeding her daydreaming rather than the other way around.

It's also possible that some maladaptive daydreamers are being misdiagnosed with mental-health conditions they don't have, due to the low awareness of maladaptive daydreaming among mental-health professionals.

Unfortunately, until more research is done, it's not possible to say whether maladaptive daydreaming is the cause or the result of poor mental health. It's probably a bit of both. It's also likely that rather than one condition directly causing the other, both might be the result of an underlying issue. For example, if you have poor social skills, you might find social situations stressful, leading to social anxiety. You might also feel lonely because you have few friends, which could cause depression. And you might try to compensate for your lack of friends by spending more time with your daydream characters, resulting in maladaptive daydreaming. The anxiety, depression and maladaptive daydreaming haven't caused each other; all of them result from the lack of social skills. And social skills can be learned.

MANAGING MALADAPTIVE DAYDREAMING ALONGSIDE OTHER CONDITIONS

If you have several conditions that result from one underlying problem, treating the underlying problem is usually the best approach. Therapy can be helpful in untangling the complicated relationships between different problems, as we'll see in Chapter 8.

In Chapter 9, we'll look at why addressing your other conditions alongside your maladaptive daydreaming is so important. If you're battling multiple problems, your mental and emotional resources will be divided. If you get help for your anxiety, depression or whatever condition you suffer from, you'll have more energy available to manage your daydreaming.

Let's look in detail at how other conditions can interact with maladaptive daydreaming.

ADHD

Over three-quarters of maladaptive daydreamers meet the criteria for a diagnosis of ADHD (Somer et al., 2017a). And around 20% of people with ADHD have symptoms of maladaptive daydreaming (Theodor-Katz et al., 2022). That's much higher than the rate of maladaptive daydreaming in the general population, which is thought to be around 2.5%.

What's going on here? Is maladaptive daydreaming a symptom of ADHD? Or does having ADHD mean you're more likely to be an immersive daydreamer or to develop maladaptive daydreaming?

Whether there's a connection between immersive daydreaming and ADHD isn't known. The research hasn't been done. It's possible that people with ADHD might be more likely than average to be immersive daydreamers. But it's also possible that immersive daydreaming is more likely to become maladaptive in people who have ADHD. In his book *Scattered Minds*, Gabor Maté discusses the connection between childhood trauma and ADHD. And, as we saw in Chapter 3, maladaptive daydreaming is often associated with childhood trauma. So it may be that ADHD and maladaptive daydreaming have a common origin, rather than either directly causing the other.

WHY ADHD MIGHT MAKE YOUR DAYDREAMING MALADAPTIVE

People with ADHD are often hypersensitive to rejection. It's called rejection sensitivity dysphoria (RSD). Almost every real-life friendship will involve an argument or misunderstanding at some point, and navigating that when you have RSD can be difficult. Daydream friendships, on the other hand, are simpler and more predictable. It's easy to see why someone with RSD might prefer an idealized daydream friendship over a complicated, unpredictable, real-life one.

Living with ADHD is tough. People with ADHD are frequently criticized for being lazy or unmotivated. Their impulsivity and inability to focus often get them in trouble, particularly in childhood, when conforming to expected behaviour in a school system designed for neurotypicals may be a challenge too far. Navigating the world as a neurodivergent person can, in itself, be a source of trauma.

Even if nothing overtly traumatic happened in childhood, it's easy to see why immersive daydreamers with ADHD might develop maladaptive daydreaming disorder.

It's also possible that some people with immersive or maladaptive daydreaming are misdiagnosed as having ADHD. The diagnostic criteria for ADHD were drawn up before maladaptive daydreaming was recognized. So the questions on ADHD screening tests weren't designed to filter out maladaptive daydreamers. Teachers and caregivers see only that a child has difficulty focussing on the task in front of them. What they can't see is whether that difficulty arises from ADHD distractibility or from a maladaptive daydreamer's need to focus on their daydream world.

JENNA'S EXPERIENCE

Jenna was diagnosed with ADHD at the age of 12. She told me what it's like having both ADHD and maladaptive daydreaming.

"A lot of people with ADHD have hyperfocuses. When I was younger, of course there was the daydreaming, but also I could sit and draw for hours and hours and not get bored. Even now, if I'm in one of those zones – with the daydreaming too – if someone's trying to talk to me, it takes a moment for them to even get my attention because I'm so there. Daydreaming is something that a lot of ADHD people can just hyperfocus on and get lost in.

"But there's also a physical aspect to it: walking, pacing, moving my hands a lot. It's not an inactive task. For the average person, if they're daydreaming, they're sitting still, maybe in a meeting or something. But for someone who immersively daydreams, there's some physicality to it. And I wonder if there's a connection with ADHD. Not everyone is physically hyperactive but a lot of people are, even if it's just twitching or shaking a leg. So your mind is super busy and you're physically moving at the same time. It makes sense to me that the two things go together.

"When I daydream, my mind is calm, even though it's very active. I think it's because you're just so in that place. And when you have ADHD, if you're engaged in something that you actually want to be engaged in or that holds your attention for a long period of time, that's appealing."

So for Jenna, daydreaming is something she hyperfocusses on. Many people with ADHD can fixate on one thing for hours, to the exclusion of all else. And in Jenna's case, one of the things she can fixate on is daydreaming. It's not that she gets distracted and mind-wanders. As we saw in Chapter 1, immersive and maladaptive daydreaming are different from mind-wandering.

Jenna also sees a connection between her daydreaming and the impulsivity that's often part of ADHD. In her daydream world, her impulsivity doesn't get her into trouble. It's a refreshing contrast to the real world, where Jenna, and other people with ADHD, often find themselves regretting an impulsive comment or action.

"My impulsivity gets me in trouble so much, but it doesn't get me in trouble in my daydream world. Because I'm planning out how I'm talking to people, or what I'm saying or how my characters react, and things like that. In the real world, I really struggle with communicating with people I don't know very well, and not saying too much, or knowing what to say, or even just holding focus in a conversation with them. That's not an issue in the daydream world because I get to control everything. And if it doesn't go the way I want, I just fix it. I recreate it in a different way, or start over, or erase it. And you can't do that in the real world.

"So it's not that being impulsive creates the daydreaming. The daydreaming is a workaround for the frustrations that come with constantly being impulsive and knowing that you say things that come out the wrong way, or you do something without thinking and then later regret it."

Depression

Two-thirds of maladaptive daydreamers suffer from depression (Somer et al., 2017a). It isn't known whether maladaptive daydreaming causes depression or maladaptive daydreaming and depression have common causes. It's likely to be a bit of both.

ARE THERE COMMON CAUSES?

In his TEDx Talk, "The Anatomy of Melancholy – Can Depression Be Good for You?" (2012), the psychiatrist and philosopher Dr Neel Burton says that people develop depression because "their world was simply not good enough for them". In other words, when real life doesn't give us what we need, depression can be a warning sign that something needs to change. But for daydreamers, when real life doesn't give us what we need, we turn to our daydreams to meet that need. And when our daydreaming meets a need that isn't being met anywhere else, we start to *need* our daydreams. And that's when daydreaming can become maladaptive.

If depression is a message that something is wrong with our lives, and maladaptive daydreaming is the way we avoid dealing with that, it's easy to see how one feeds on the other. But ultimately, both conditions are signals that real life is not meeting all of our needs.

Another function of depression is to remove us from a stressful situation. When we're depressed, we don't feel like doing anything. We withdraw from the world. It's how we try to protect ourselves from further stress. Maladaptive daydreaming does the same thing: it prompts us to withdraw from the real world to somewhere that feels safer.

CAN MALADAPTIVE DAYDREAMING CAUSE DEPRESSION?

As you can see, there are several reasons why someone might develop both depression *and* maladaptive daydreaming in response to the same event or situation. However, there are also ways that maladaptive daydreaming might cause depression.

First, the time we spend daydreaming is time we're not spending living in reality – maintaining friendships, having fun, progressing our careers – and this can lead to becoming socially isolated and generally stagnating. We see the people around us moving forward while we're stuck in a mundane, uninspiring existence where nothing ever changes. It's easy to see why that might make us depressed.

Second, we might view ourselves as weak or defective because we can't stop daydreaming. Our inner critic takes over and tells us that if we cared more, tried harder or were just generally a better person, we'd be able to put the daydreaming aside and get on with life. Hopefully, by now, you're realizing that's not true. But if you've judged yourself harshly for being a daydreamer, you probably don't like yourself much, and depression can be the way you express that.

Third, if our idealized daydream relationships have given us unrealistic expectations of what a real-life relationship can or should be, we might feel that people are constantly letting us down or that we'll never find friends or a partner who is as perfect as our daydream characters.

Finally, if we become an idealized version of ourself in our daydreams, then comparing our real-world self to our daydream self can bring up some difficult emotions. If we see our daydream self as an unattainable fantasy, we might become self-critical of the person we are in real life.

MY EXPERIENCE

I suffered from depression on and off for over 20 years. Hormonal fluctuations made it worse. I experienced antenatal depression during both my pregnancies. With my first pregnancy, my mood lifted soon after my twin daughters were born. But when my son was born a few years later, my antenatal depression was followed by postnatal depression. All of my children are IVF babies, so it was difficult to admit I was miserable when I'd been blessed with three children I thought I'd never have. Mums with postnatal depression don't always have trouble bonding with their children. I connected with my son the minute he was born. I had so much love for him. But life with a new baby was hard. It felt as though he barely slept. By the time he was five months old, I was exhausted. He'd be up several times every night, and it was difficult to settle him back down. And if he ever napped during the day, instead of catching up on my own sleep, I prioritized spending time with my daughters. I felt as if I was sleep-walking through life. The real world became a blur. But my daydreams came alive.

I lost count of the hours in the middle of the night that I spent sitting in the dark feeding my son, or waiting for him to fall asleep, or waiting for him to be in a deep enough sleep that I could risk moving him back to his cot. If I tried to put him down too soon, he'd wake up and I'd have to start all over again. I had a lot of time when there was nothing to do but sit and think. And I didn't want to think about how exhausting and difficult my life had become. I felt guilty for even feeling like that when I'd had three children through the miracle that is IVF. So I did what I always do when things get difficult. I mentally checked out.

There was a house for sale at the time, about ten miles from where we lived, out in the countryside. It had four acres of land, and the ominous lack of photographs on the estate agent's website suggested it needed work. It cost twice what we could have realistically afforded. The location would have been utterly impractical. It wasn't near any good schools. I'm not the sort of person who would ever take on a renovation project. And I don't know what we would have done with all that land. But for some reason I loved that house.

And so in my daydreams we bought it. We kept chickens and goats. We grew all our own vegetables, and I started my own business. Not having photographs of the interior meant I was free to design it exactly how I wanted. And I did, right down to the furniture. There was a huge entrance hall, with terracotta tiles on the floor, and high ceilings. In December, we'd set up an enormous Christmas tree with sparkly lights, and there'd be an open fire in the living room. I was joyful and vibrant and full of energy. My children were healthy and happy and spent their time outdoors instead of on screens. It was an idyllic life, and imagining it got me through the exhausting reality of nappies, baby food, crying, school runs and never ever enough sleep.

This illustrates the contradiction that maladaptive daydreaming so often is. On the one hand, my daydreams were a lifeline. If I hadn't been able to mentally check out during all those hours in the middle of the night, sitting quietly in the dark holding my sleeping son, I think I'd have gone crazy. My daydreams were most definitely meeting a need. But they also spilled over into my day and made me less present in the precious moments I had with my children. And as my son's sleep gradually improved, the daydreams proved hard to give up. It was only when I started practising mindfulness that I was able to get my daydreaming back under control. We'll come back to the topic of mindfulness, and why it can be so helpful in managing maladaptive daydreaming, in Chapter 10.

Anxiety

It's thought that 30% of people suffer from some form of anxiety. But among maladaptive daydreamers that proportion rises to over 70% (Somer et al., 2017a). If you're an immersive daydreamer with anxiety, there are several reasons why your daydreaming might become maladaptive.

First, anxiety feels horrible. You might have physical symptoms – a tightening in your chest, feeling your heart pounding or racing, or a nauseous sensation in your stomach. You might also have repetitive or intrusive negative thoughts. It's natural to want to get away from those unpleasant symptoms. And one way you can do that is by daydreaming. Daydreaming distracts you from intrusive thoughts, and it also disconnects you from your body so you can ignore those uncomfortable physical sensations.

Second, daydreaming gives you a sense of control. Most anxiety stems from uncertainty – being afraid of what might happen, because you can't completely control the outcome. But in your daydreams, you can control everything. You can either use your daydreaming as an escape, by making your daydream world a refuge where the thing you're anxious about simply doesn't exist, or you can use your daydream world as a safe space to rehearse possible outcomes. You can imagine the worst and think about how you'd manage it. That can help you feel more prepared and therefore more in control.

Third, if you have social anxiety, the unpredictability of real-life relationships can be terrifying. You might constantly worry what other people think of you or be always on guard in case you accidentally upset someone. Daydream relationships feel safer because you're in control and there's no fear of rejection or misunderstanding.

Maladaptive daydreaming that's triggered by anxiety can take on a life of its own. It's an effective way to relieve anxiety in the moment, and it's always available, so it's easy to get into the habit of daydreaming whenever you feel anxious. But over time, the gap between feeling anxious and starting to daydream gets smaller and smaller until eventually your conscious mind isn't even aware of the anxiety. All you know is that you're suddenly in a daydream. And because you're not allowing yourself to feel the anxiety, you might forget you have it or think it's gone away. So it's not unusual for maladaptive daydreaming to be covering underlying anxiety that you're not even aware of. That's what happened to Mia.

MIA'S EXPERIENCE

Mia had probably been using her daydreaming to cover her anxiety for a while, but things got worse after she became a parent. She started having disturbing daydreams of a kind she'd never experienced before.

"I think that I was getting normal parental anxiety and fears, and in a normal person they would freak you out but then pass. You'd be able to rationalize it away. But for me they were filtered through my capacity for intense daydreaming, so what they turned into were these vivid, prolonged and persistent fantasies of some guy running up to us on the playground and kidnapping my son and selling him into sex slavery. And what if I bring a gun and then I shoot the bad guy? But I missed and I shot my baby. That kind of stuff.

"These weird intrusive daydreams weren't like my normal ones. My normal ones are just stupid fantasy adventures. They're fun. They can be weird and violent, but they're fun. These were a completely different beast. I would make a conscious effort to be like, ignore those thoughts, go into your fantasy land."

I asked her if she used her fun daydreams as a coping mechanism for the horrible intrusive daydreams.

"Yeah, I was like, I know this hole. I get sucked into this hole all the time. Let's go down the good rabbit hole."

Mia shared her experience on a parenting forum, and another parent advised her to treat her intrusive daydreams like intrusive thoughts. She went online and researched strategies to manage intrusive thoughts, and the intrusive daydreams subsided. As they did, her normal daydreaming started to come back, but because she wanted to be more present with her son, she decided to work on reducing that too. And that's when she noticed the anxiety.

"When the intrusive daydreaming subsided, my normal daydreaming was coming back as it always had, but I was actively working on lessening that too. And I was just anxious all the time. Maybe the anxiety started when I became a parent. I never noticed it until I started reducing my maladaptive daydreaming, but I never bothered to reduce my maladaptive daydreaming until I had a child. So, I don't know."

"But you noticed that as you reduced the daydreaming, the anxiety came up?"

"The anxiety bubbled up, yeah. I went to my doctor, and she gave me a prescription and sent me to a therapist."

"And did that help?" I asked.

"No. I think the prescription did a bit. But it also completely suppressed my sex drive, and we were trying to conceive, so I just stopped taking it. And therapy was OK, but I didn't really get much out of it. I don't know what I was expecting. I felt like I mostly just sat there and talked at her about all kinds of random stuff. I derailed us a lot and she never got us back on track. So I stopped going. It was too expensive."

Mia is learning to live with her anxiety. She's found that prioritizing healthy sleep habits helps her control both her anxiety and her maladaptive daydreaming.

"When I was reducing maladaptive daydreaming, part of it was to sleep better. I think sleep deprivation had a bigger impact than anybody gave it credit for. Maladaptive daydreaming is a lot easier to control when you're well rested, and I was never well rested. I would daydream all night, drifting in and out of fitful sleep, and daydreaming the rest of the night, all through the night. And then try to go about my day running on nothing. For years I did that. So, I put a lot of effort into sleeping better, and I think that it helped everything, the maladaptive daydreaming and the anxiety."

I asked Mia how she sees the relationship between maladaptive daydreaming and anxiety.

"I think maladaptive daydreaming caused my anxiety. I've got no expertise to back that up. It's just what I think happened. Having my brain work that way for years, and not learning any other coping skills, not learning to emotionally regulate, not building all those healthy pathways in my brain, I think left the door wide open for other diagnoses to come in.

"So maladaptive daydreaming caused the anxiety, or at least led to the circumstances that caused it, but I also think it hid it for a long time after I had it. I don't think I noticed I had it, because I don't know when my thoughts transitioned from normal anxiousness to disordered anxiousness. My maladaptive daydreaming was already covering the normal anxiousness, so it was a very short step to cover the disordered anxiousness. And it did. It is a good coping skill. It is good enough that I don't even notice it most of the time. I think before I'm even registering that I'm feeling anxious, it's already winding up. So I think they go hand in hand."

Mia's experience with anxiety mirrors my experience with depression. When you don't have healthy coping skills and you don't know how to regulate your emotions, you're vulnerable to a range of mental-health problems. And maladaptive daydreaming becomes the way you try to manage poor mental health. But as we saw in Chapter 4, it can cause as many problems as it solves.

You can't address maladaptive daydreaming in isolation

As we've seen, the majority of maladaptive daydreamers have one or more coexisting conditions. That's why it's important to take a holistic approach to overcoming maladaptive daydreaming. If you try to stop daydreaming without recognizing and addressing the underlying issue, it's going to resurface. And if the only way you know how to deal with it is by daydreaming, it's going to be hard to keep your daydreaming under control.

If you have other conditions in addition to your maladaptive daydreaming, I urge you to talk to your doctor if you haven't already. Depression and anxiety can be treated, and by getting them under control, you free up mental and emotional resources that you can use to tackle your maladaptive daydreaming.

We've covered a lot in this first part of the book. You've learned what immersive and maladaptive daydreaming are, where you fall on the immersive–maladaptive spectrum and why your daydreaming might have originally become maladaptive. We've also looked at the ways in which your maladaptive daydreaming is harming you.

Although your maladaptive daydreaming isn't your fault, healing from it is your responsibility. In Part 2, we're going to walk through the four steps you need to take to sustainably overcome your maladaptive daydreaming.

PART 2

HOW TO OVERCOME MALADAPTIVE DAYDREAMING

PART 2

HOW TO OVERCOME MALADAPTIVE DAYDREAMING

CHAPTER 6

PREPARING FOR HEALING

In Part 1 of this book, we looked at what immersive and maladaptive daydreaming are, and we took a deep dive into understanding maladaptive daydreaming – how it starts, how it can harm us and what other mental-health conditions it can be associated with. In this part, we'll look in detail at how you can manage, and eventually heal from, your maladaptive daydreaming.

You probably bought this book because you've realized that maladaptive daydreaming isn't something you can just decide to stop doing. It's never as simple as realizing this habit is harming you and resolving not to do it anymore. If it was that easy, you'd have done it a long time ago. But the reality is that changing habits is hard. And breaking an addiction to your own thoughts is even harder.

It's essential to approach this in the right way. Do not dive into this impulsively. You can't just decide to stop daydreaming and expect to be successful. You need to prepare yourself and your life to give you the best chance of overcoming your maladaptive daydreaming.

This book will give you a sustainable and compassionate way to turn your maladaptive daydreaming into immersive daydreaming. Overcoming maladaptive daydreaming doesn't mean that you stop daydreaming completely. Daydreaming is a fundamental part of who you are. You don't need to – and in fact you shouldn't – suppress it. But you do need to stop it taking over your life.

The four steps to overcoming maladaptive daydreaming

The reason this book can help you when your previous attempts to overcome maladaptive daydreaming have failed is that you won't be addressing your maladaptive daydreaming in isolation. You won't even address it first. Before you can heal from maladaptive daydreaming, you have to have some other things in place.

As we saw in Part 1, your maladaptive daydreaming began as your mind's attempt to solve a problem. Your daydreaming may now be so out of control that it's causing serious problems of its own, but it started as a way of dealing with something that you didn't know how to deal with any other way. Before you can heal from maladaptive daydreaming, you have to have resolved the underlying problem that drove you into maladaptive daydreaming in the first place. You need to be absolutely clear about that: *if the original problem has not been solved, you will not be able to stop daydreaming.*

The second thing you have to do before you can heal from maladaptive daydreaming is decide what you're going to replace it with. And I don't just mean you need a healthier coping mechanism to help you deal with the problems that life will inevitably throw at you. I mean you need to have something to fill all of the time you're currently spending daydreaming. If your maladaptive daydreaming has been a problem for a long time, most of your real-life activities have probably been squeezed out to make space for it. Daydreaming is likely the only thing in life that gives you any real enjoyment. Take that away, and where will you be?

That's why you shouldn't try to stop or even cut down on your daydreaming in isolation. If you take away your coping mechanism, especially when that's the only thing that gives you any real pleasure in life, you're left with a dull, dreary, mundane life and no way to cope with the negative emotions that will inevitably result from that. That's a perfect recipe to drive you straight back into daydreaming. And if, by some miracle, you resist the urge to daydream, your mind will search for other ways to cope, other ways to numb out the pain, and you'll likely fall into some other addictive behaviour. So it's imperative that you break this addiction in the right way: by understanding what need your daydreaming is meeting and by making sure that your real life is a place you want to come back to *before* you try to tackle the daydreaming.

Before you do any of that, there is one more thing you have to do. You have to like yourself. You have to believe that you deserve to be free of maladaptive daydreaming. You have to believe that you are worthy of a great life in the real world. And to do that, you have to release the shame you feel about being a maladaptive daydreamer. When you can accept being a daydreamer as part of who you are, without seeing yourself as broken, defective or in any way *less than*, you'll be better able to work on creating the life you want to live. And when you can see your daydreaming as a problem you're struggling with, rather than a defect you have, it will be easier to ask the people closest to you for support.

To overcome your maladaptive daydreaming, we'll work through the following steps:

1. We'll tackle the shame you feel about being a daydreamer.
2. We'll look at what problem your daydreaming is attempting to solve and how you can solve that problem in a healthier way.
3. We'll discuss how you can make your real life a place you want to come back to.
4. Only after steps 1–3 will we finally look at strategies to help you take control of your daydreaming. If you try to attack your daydreaming without having the other pieces in place, you're basically going to war with yourself, and that will just make the whole process much harder.

This isn't going to be easy. It isn't going to happen overnight. And I can't do it for you. I can show you how, but, ultimately, you're going to have to take responsibility for your own healing. And that's a daunting task. So before we start, I want to help you get clear about why you want to heal from maladaptive daydreaming and what relationship you want to have with your daydreaming in the future. I'll also introduce you to some of the sources of support you may need as you undertake this journey.

The ultimate goal: immersive daydreaming

Let's begin by getting one thing clear. Your goal shouldn't be to stop daydreaming completely. In my opinion, that's both unrealistic and unhealthy. The only way you're going to overcome your maladaptive daydreaming is if every part of you wants to heal and every part of you believes you can. If those two conditions are not met, the parts of you that don't want to change or don't believe you can change will resist the process. They will fight with the parts of you that want to heal, and you will sabotage your own efforts.

Regardless of how much damage your maladaptive daydreaming is doing to your life, the chances are there are aspects of your daydreaming that you enjoy – the excitement of working out a new plot twist, or spending time with that special character you're genuinely in love with. It's completely natural that you don't want to give those up. If you think that overcoming maladaptive daydreaming means you have to stop daydreaming completely, and you don't want to give up your daydream world and your characters, you're not going to be committed to healing, because there's a part of you that doesn't want to be healed.

Similarly, if you've tried to stop daydreaming many times before and you've failed every time, there will be a part of you that believes that overcoming maladaptive daydreaming isn't possible. You'll wonder whether there's any point trying again. Why would the outcome be different this time? Why invest time and energy in something that isn't going to work?

But what if you don't have to stop completely? As we saw in Part 1, all maladaptive daydreamers start out as immersive daydreamers. You were an immersive daydreamer once. You can be again. Immersive daydreaming doesn't have any of the negative consequences of maladaptive daydreaming. As an immersive daydreamer, you can control your daydreaming. You can choose to stop daydreaming when you have something more important to do. You can check in with your characters whenever you want without being dependent on them. You can *choose* to daydream instead of *needing* to daydream.

Why immersive daydreaming?

There's a big difference between maladaptive daydreaming, which is a destructive behavioural addiction that stops you from fully living your real life, and immersive daydreaming, which is a natural thinking style that you can learn to use as a powerful tool to enhance your real life. Understanding this distinction is crucial to understanding what we mean by overcoming maladaptive daydreaming. What we need to overcome is the maladaptive part, not the daydreaming part.

The problems caused by maladaptive daydreaming aren't caused by the act of daydreaming itself; they arise because we don't have enough control over our daydreaming. We daydream when we should be doing other things. We use our daydreaming to run away from our problems. If we can stop doing that, we turn daydreaming into an entertaining hobby that we indulge in only when we can genuinely spare the time. That's immersive daydreaming, and there's nothing wrong with it.

If one of the things that has been holding you back from tackling your maladaptive daydreaming is a fear of having to say goodbye to characters and worlds that mean a great deal to you, don't worry. You won't be saying goodbye to anything unless and until you feel it's right for you.

Another reason I don't recommend trying to stop daydreaming completely is that your daydreaming is part of who you are. It's how you think. You were born an immersive daydreamer. Right now, you may equate being a daydreamer with being "broken" or "defective", but we're going to work on that. I hope that by the time you finish this book, you'll see that being an immersive daydreamer can be a beautiful gift. But even if you can't see it that way, remember that being a daydreamer is not something you have a choice about.

In Part 1, we saw how maladaptive daydreamers can lose connection with themselves. This results both from the trauma that often underlies maladaptive daydreaming and from years of telling ourselves that our daydreams – and therefore our daydream selves – aren't real. Losing your sense of self, not knowing who you really are, can contribute to a whole range of mental-health problems. To be truly mentally healthy, you have to get to know and love your authentic self. You cannot truly love yourself if you're repressing a part of yourself that you're not comfortable with.

Being a daydreamer is part of what makes you the unique person that you are. You can try to repress it, but it isn't going away. And as long as you repress it, you will never find the inner peace you need to stay mentally well.

What does healthy immersive daydreaming look like?

Before you start the hard work of overcoming your maladaptive daydreaming, you need to be clear about what immersive daydreaming means to you. In other words, you need to understand, in detail, what healthy daydreaming looks like in the context of *your* life. You're going to have to do a bit of work here because the definition of healthy daydreaming is different for everyone. I can't tell you what's healthy for you. But don't panic; the worksheet that accompanies this chapter can help you.

HOW MUCH TIME CAN YOU SPEND DAYDREAMING BEFORE IT BECOMES UNHEALTHY?

When you're considering what healthy daydreaming means for you, there are a few things to think about. The first is how much time you can afford to spend daydreaming each day, and that's a personal decision. What might be a healthy and reasonable amount of time for one person could be unrealistic for someone with different life circumstances. You'll need to strike a balance. You need to reduce your daydreaming enough that you have time for all the things you want to do in real life. But if you try to reduce it too much, you could end up constantly fighting an urge to daydream, which will just make your recovery more difficult. I encourage you to try to set a specific amount of time you would ideally like to daydream each day. You can always adjust it as you go along if it becomes clear that your original allocation isn't working. But if you have a specific numerical target in mind, it will give you something concrete to aim at, and you'll be able to measure your progress against a defined goal.

You should also think about when you can fit daydreaming into your day without it being too much of a problem. For example, you might decide it's OK to daydream on the bus on the way home from work, because there's nothing much else you can do with that time. Or you might feel that you can set aside an hour just before you go to bed as a reward for being productive during the day. Or, conversely, you might want to avoid daydreaming after a certain time in the evening because it tempts you to stay up late and makes it hard to establish healthy sleep habits. You have to think about what's going to work *for you*.

HEALTHY DAYDREAMING DOESN'T MAKE YOU FEEL BAD

The total amount of time you spend daydreaming isn't the only indication of whether your daydreaming is immersive or maladaptive. You also have to consider how your daydreaming makes you feel. When you have a healthy relationship with your daydreaming, you shouldn't feel any shame about being a daydreamer. If you see your daydreaming as a sign that you're somehow defective or broken, it's going to be difficult to have a healthy relationship with it. As you transition to immersive daydreaming, you'll need to accept that being a daydreamer is part of who you are and that learning to love your daydreaming is just as important as learning to love any other aspect of yourself.

HEALTHY DAYDREAMING IS MOTIVATIONAL RATHER THAN ESCAPIST

Another thing to consider as you transition to immersive daydreaming is that you'll need to bring your real life and your daydream life into balance. This is partly about reducing your daydreaming so that you leave time for real life, but it's also about accepting that if you want to have a real life that's worth living, you have to work at it. You'll need to decide what you want out of life and take action to make it happen. Healthy immersive daydreaming can help you with that. We'll dive into this in detail in Chapter 9, but it's worth starting to think about some of the things you'd like to do once you get your daydreaming under control.

Healthy daydreaming shouldn't be unavoidably triggered by anything. For most of the common daydream triggers, it's neither healthy nor desirable to avoid the trigger forever. For example, if you're triggered by music, then one of the indications of healthy daydreaming might be that you can listen to music without feeling an urge to daydream. We'll look more at triggers and how to manage them in Chapter 10.

HEALTHY DAYDREAMING IS A CHOICE

In my opinion, one of the clearest indications that you've made the transition to immersive daydreaming is when you can honestly say that you daydream because you *want* to rather than because you *have* to. In other words, you've let go of the addictive part of your daydreaming and you're now able to see it as a hobby or a motivational tool. At the moment, your daydreaming feels addictive because it's meeting your need to escape from something. When you don't need to escape, you won't *need* to daydream.

It's OK to ask for help

Before we start looking at how to manage your maladaptive daydreaming, I want to emphasize that you don't have to do this alone. Maladaptive daydreaming is a mental-health problem, and, like any mental-health problem, you'll overcome it more easily if you have support. Most daydreamers find it intensely embarrassing to talk about their daydreaming, so the idea of asking someone, especially a mental-health professional, to help you overcome your maladaptive daydreaming can be daunting. But there is help available if you can find the courage to ask for it.

Let's look at the types of professional support you might consider.

MEDICATION

Medication has a role to play in many mental-health conditions, so why not maladaptive daydreaming? Unfortunately, studies that have looked at the effect of medication on daydreaming have been inconclusive (Ross et al., 2020). There doesn't seem to be any medication that consistently improves maladaptive daydreaming in everyone who takes it. But, anecdotally, some daydreamers report that certain medications make it easier for them to control their daydreaming. Two things that some people find helpful are antidepressants and stimulants.

I have personally taken three different antidepressants over the course of my life, and none of them made the slightest bit of difference to my daydreaming. But everyone's experience is different. As we have seen, Alice uses daydreaming to cope with the effects of poor mental health, but she's also open to using medication when necessary. She found that antidepressants changed the quality of her daydreaming: "I've tried quite a few SSRIs, and I felt some emotional numbing on them for a while. It affected my daydreams. Because our daydreams are emotionally charged for most of us, so if the medications are numbing you emotionally, your daydreams aren't going to feel as full of energy."

Until scientists understand why medications affect people differently, all you can do is persuade your doctor to let you try. Approach medication as an experiment. Some daydreamers find that ADHD medications, for example, increase their ability to focus on *everything*, including daydreaming. So don't be afraid to go back to your doctor if it doesn't work.

Jenna, who we met in Chapter 5, had been managing her ADHD without medication for several years, but chose to go back on medication when she realized she was struggling at work. However, it didn't help her manage her daydreaming. Jenna explained: "I was really struggling at the beginning of last school year. My coworker across the hall has ADHD and she said I might need to go back on medicine. And I was like, well, OK, maybe a positive side effect would be it could help with the daydreaming. So, I got back on the medicine, and it helped the work situation a lot. But I can't say that it affects the daydreaming at all."

MEDICATION IS WORTH CONSIDERING EVEN IF IT DOESN'T AFFECT YOUR DAYDREAMING

Even if medication doesn't affect your daydreaming, it may be helpful in treating a coexisting condition. As we saw in Chapter 5, 75% of maladaptive daydreamers meet the criteria for ADHD, and two-thirds struggle with depression. If you are depressed and maladaptively daydreaming, you have two mountains to climb. If antidepressants help you manage your depression, you'll have more energy to tackle your daydreaming. Mental health is rarely one thing in isolation. By addressing any coexisting mental-health problems, you're giving yourself the best chance of overcoming your maladaptive daydreaming.

However, if you do find a medication that works for you, please be careful. As I mentioned above, I've taken antidepressants when I've needed to. I'm not anti-medication. Antidepressants have lifted me out of some dark places, but they are not a cure for depression. When I was so depressed I didn't want to recover, medication lifted me to a place where I could do the work to get better. I've had depressive episodes that I wouldn't have survived without medication. But medication didn't solve my problems. It's a coping mechanism, just like daydreaming. If you use medication to get you to a place where you can do the work, it's healthy. If you expect medication to do the work for you, it isn't. Use medication as a tool to assist you on this journey if it helps you, but please don't see it as a substitute for following the rest of the strategies in this book.

THERAPY

Another thing that many maladaptive daydreamers consider is therapy. This could be counselling, where you talk one-to-one with a professional about the issues that are most important to you. Or it could be a skills-based therapy, such as cognitive behavioural therapy (CBT) or dialectical behavioural therapy (DBT), where you learn skills that will help you better navigate life's challenges. I believe therapy can be a significant part of the treatment for maladaptive daydreaming, and if it's available and affordable for you, I'd strongly advise you to look into it.

TALKING TO YOUR DOCTOR

If you think either medication or therapy is something you'd like to explore, you'll need to talk to your doctor. And that can be a scary prospect if you've never told anyone about your daydreaming. You might wonder how you're going to explain what's going on in your head without sounding crazy. You might worry that your doctor won't take you seriously. Or you might be terrified that they'll ask you what you daydream about.

Jenna's doctor was sceptical when she initially told him about her maladaptive daydreaming. But when she insisted that she needed help, she eventually got his attention and he referred her for therapy. Jenna told me: "When I first told him, he just looked at me. And then I tried to explain it to him and he said, 'Oh, so this is just something you came up with on your own?' And I'm like, 'No, you're not listening to me.' And so I explained it to him again, and he jotted something down. And then he said, 'So you just diagnosed yourself with this?' and then I just left, pissed off. But the next time I went in, he asked me more questions about it. So, although his attitude toward it the first time was very off-putting, he did think about it. And then he asked more about it, and that's when he referred me to the therapist that works in his office."

HOW TO NAVIGATE YOUR FIRST DOCTOR'S APPOINTMENT

If Jenna's experience sounds scary, don't panic. There are things you can do to make that initial doctor's appointment flow smoothly. First, do some preparation. If you can, send your doctor some information about maladaptive daydreaming in advance or print something out to take with you if you can't contact the doctor beforehand. Search the internet for a brief article that explains maladaptive daydreaming in a way that resonates with you. I've included links to a couple of articles in the Resources section. I also recommend giving your doctor a link to the ICMDR website, where they can see the scientific research that's been done into maladaptive daydreaming.

Second, download the MDS-16 from the ICMDR website and score yourself on it. This will give your doctor some evidence that what you're suffering from *is* maladaptive daydreaming. You should also make a list of the *specific* ways that your daydreaming is harming you. If you find it hard to be specific, look back at Chapter 4 for ideas.

Then, when you see the doctor, you'll be in a great position to quickly explain what maladaptive daydreaming is, show that you're suffering from it and explain how it's affecting you and why you need help with it. Then you need to ask for what you want – if you want to try antidepressants or stimulants, say so. If you want to try therapy, ask for a referral. Don't feel pressured to talk about the content of your daydreams if you don't want to. It's not relevant in a first appointment. If the doctor asks, you can simply say that your daydreams are creative fantasies that aren't related to events in real life. You can talk about the *quality* of your daydreams instead of the *content*. Say that you can remain focussed on the same scene for hours at a time, or that you've been developing the same plot for months. It's things like that which differentiate maladaptive daydreaming from mind-wandering or rumination, which are the things your doctor needs to rule out.

TAKING RESPONSIBILITY FOR YOUR HEALING

What if you don't feel ready to talk to your doctor? Or if medication isn't for you? Or if therapy is too expensive or not widely available where you live? Unfortunately, that's the reality for many maladaptive daydreamers. And so, although I urge you to seek support from your doctor if you possibly can, I have written this book to help you work on your maladaptive daydreaming without professional support if that's your only option.

That brings me to a crucial point: your daydreaming is happening in your head, and the only person who can control what goes on in there is you. Ultimately, if you're going to overcome maladaptive daydreaming, you're going to have to take responsibility for it. No one else is going to do the work for you. Even if you go to therapy, the therapist can't force you to think differently. That's something you have to commit to doing for yourself. Your mental health is your responsibility.

That can feel unfair, especially if you now understand why your daydreaming became maladaptive in the first place. Because hopefully you can see that it's not your fault that you have maladaptive daydreaming. You didn't choose to have the immersive daydreaming trait. You didn't choose to experience the trauma that made your daydreaming maladaptive. You didn't choose to become addicted to your fantasy world.

But just because you didn't create this situation doesn't mean you can't take responsibility for fixing it. And when it comes to your mental health, that's exactly what you have to do. It might feel unfair that you have to take responsibility for fixing a problem you didn't create, but it can also be empowering. Because no matter what circumstances led to you developing maladaptive daydreaming, you have the ability to overcome it.

You have a choice. You can choose to keep running away to a world that can never be real, or you can choose to take the parts of that world that mean something to you and figure out how to get the same sense of meaning and purpose in real life. In the following chapters, I'll show you how to do that.

If you take one thing away from this chapter, it should be this: overcoming maladaptive daydreaming will not be quick; it will not be easy; you will have to be committed and determined, and you will have to be brutally honest with yourself about the effect your daydreaming is having on your life. *But you can do it. And it will be worth it.*

The importance of self-monitoring

We're going to end this chapter with something you can do right now to start you on the path toward overcoming maladaptive daydreaming.

When you commit to making any kind of change in your life, it's essential that you define where you're starting from, where you want to get to, and how you're going to know whether you're making progress. Overcoming maladaptive daydreaming is no different.

The tool you use to track your progress is self-monitoring. Self-monitoring is simple. All you need to do is record every day how many times you daydreamed, how long you daydreamed for, any factors that prompted you to start or continue daydreaming and how you felt when you stopped daydreaming. Below, I've included a link to a basic form that you can use to record your daydreaming activities each day, but please feel free to create your own in a format that works for you. You might, for example, want to include columns to record your mood, what you were doing while you were daydreaming or any stressful events. As you become aware of your daydreaming patterns, you may think of other things you want to track, so don't feel you have to stick rigidly to any particular format. The form contains the minimum, but you can add to it in any way you find helpful.

You need to make time *every day* to record your daydreaming. Don't assume that you'll be able to remember even a couple of days later how much you daydreamed on any particular day. Daydreaming is such a natural part of our lives that we don't remember when and for how long we do it. Self-monitoring helps you change that. It will feel like a chore at first, and you'll probably feel some resistance to doing it. But stick with it. As you make it a habit, it will get easier.

At this stage, *all* you're doing is self-monitoring. You don't need to try to reduce your daydreaming. You're just getting a clear picture of your daydreaming so that you know where you're starting from. Then, when you start to tackle it in the following chapters, you'll be able to see how much progress you're making.

Example self-monitoring form

Download the form at:
https://daydreamplace.com/extreme-imagination/
self-monitoring-form.pdf

WHY SELF-MONITORING WORKS

You'll be more motivated to complete a self-monitoring form every day if you understand why you're doing it. Let's look in detail at why self-monitoring is helpful.

First, self-monitoring gives you a starting point. It's hard to estimate how much time you spend daydreaming. Time passes differently in the daydream world. We've all had the experience of being lost in a daydream and suddenly being shocked at how much time has passed. It's also difficult to appreciate how much your daydreaming varies from day to day. You know you have good days and bad days, but on a good day, you may not remember just how bad the bad days are, and vice versa. By consistently recording your daydreaming for a few weeks, you'll have a much better idea of what a typical daydreaming day looks like for you.

Second, self-monitoring allows you to track your progress. Once you start actively trying to overcome your maladaptive daydreaming, your self-monitoring forms will allow you to see how well you're doing. Being able to see your progress is a crucial part of staying motivated. Healing from any mental-health condition is not a linear process. Sometimes you will relapse. And when you do, it's easy to feel that you're back to square one, and that's when you might be tempted to give up. But if you can look back at your self-monitoring forms and see that you're making real progress, it will be easier to put any relapse into perspective and not let it derail your recovery.

Third, self-monitoring can, in itself, reduce your daydreaming. Scientific research has shown that self-monitoring alone, without taking any other action, can significantly reduce maladaptive daydreaming in some people (Herscu, 2021). Don't worry if this doesn't work for you – there are plenty of other strategies in this book, and self-monitoring is a small part of the overall picture. But if you do notice a reduction in your daydreaming just from self-monitoring, don't be surprised. Sometimes, knowing that you're going to have to record a daydream on your form can be enough to stop you from giving in to the urge. And regularly reviewing your daydreaming can make you more aware of it, which may give you more opportunity to decide not to daydream in any given moment.

Finally, self-monitoring can help you become aware of your triggers. Some daydreaming triggers are obvious – you might know that listening to a particular song will activate your daydreaming. But other triggers are more subtle. It took me a long time to realize that my biggest trigger is boredom. Writing down what was going on when you started daydreaming can help you identify triggers you weren't previously aware of.

SOLA'S EXPERIENCE OF SELF-MONITORING

Sola experimented with self-monitoring when she first decided to take control of her maladaptive daydreaming.

"The first time I felt like I really needed to get off of daydreaming, I started tracking my time really obsessively. I didn't manage to do it all day long, but I would try to track how much I was daydreaming, and I was trying really hard to get off of daydreaming."

"Were you surprised by how much time you were spending daydreaming?" I asked her.

"It was almost all my waking hours, all day long. I would do it when I was waking up, and then I would do it when I was going somewhere. When it was at its most severe, I remember in the street there's a tree every 20 metres. I remember trying to go to the next tree without daydreaming. That's just 20 metres, and I remember I couldn't do it."

"Did tracking it help you reduce how much you were daydreaming?"

"I don't think that was the crucial step. But I think at the time it was the best thing I could do, and obviously it helped with my awareness. You can track your time, and daydream, and try to get rid of it. But what I think now is that you will always be a daydreamer and you cannot get rid of daydreaming. But at the time, I think I needed to document it."

YOU DON'T NEED TO RECORD WHAT YOU DAYDREAM ABOUT

I don't recommend recording *what* you daydream about, although you can if you think it would be helpful. I personally feel uncomfortable writing down anything about what happens in my daydreams, and I don't want you to include anything on your self-monitoring form that could deter you from filling it in. As I reiterate throughout this book, it's not what you daydream about that determines whether your daydreaming is immersive or maladaptive; what matters is whether your daydreaming is helping or hindering your real life. That's what your self-monitoring sheet should reflect.

You need to make self-monitoring a habit. You should fill in self-monitoring forms every day for at least as long as you're working through the strategies outlined in this book. Ideally, you will continue until you have transitioned to immersive daydreaming. So take a moment, right now, to print out and fill in your first self-monitoring form, and then congratulate yourself. You've taken the first step toward overcoming your maladaptive daydreaming.

Worksheet: Your definition of immersive daydreaming

The worksheet that accompanies this chapter will help you start to understand what healthy immersive daydreaming looks like in the context of your life. This will give you an idea of what you're aiming at as you work through the following chapters.

Download the worksheet at:
https://daydreamplace.com/extreme-imagination/worksheet-chapter6.pdf

CHAPTER 7

OVERCOMING SHAME

Nearly all maladaptive daydreamers struggle with shame. In this chapter, we'll explore why being ashamed of your daydreaming will get in the way of you overcoming the maladaptive parts of your daydreaming. We'll also look at ways you can begin to release that shame. We'll see that the key to overcoming shame is not to change who you are, but to learn to like who you are.

Letting go of your shame allows you to make peace with your daydreaming, to accept it, even embrace it, as an integral part of who you are. Because when you make peace with your daydreaming, it tends to make peace with you.

What is shame?

Shame is the most debilitating emotion. Shame tells us we're worthless. Shame says no one likes us. Shame makes us hide. And the hardest part is that shame doesn't give us a way out. Shame doesn't encourage us to solve a problem. Instead, it convinces us we *are* the problem.

Other negative emotions motivate us to change our behaviour or our situation. Anger tells us to assert ourselves when someone violates our boundaries. Fear warns us of danger and tries to keep us safe. Guilt urges us not to repeat an action that hurt us or someone else. But shame? Shame doesn't offer a solution. It doesn't give us hope.

When we feel shame, our natural reaction is to withdraw, to hide away, to interact as little as possible with the world around us. Shame tells us that we're bad, and we don't want anyone else to see that.

WHAT'S THE DIFFERENCE BETWEEN GUILT AND SHAME?

The words "guilt" and "shame" are often used interchangeably, but they're different. Guilt is when we feel bad about something we *did*, whereas shame is when we feel bad about something we *are*. That makes guilt easier to manage. If we've behaved badly, and our actions have harmed us or someone we care about, we can resolve to do better next time. So guilt serves a purpose. It motivates us to learn from our mistakes and not repeat harmful behaviour.

If you feel guilty about how much time you've spent daydreaming, that's healthy. You're supposed to feel guilty if you were daydreaming when you should have been doing something more important. That guilt will help motivate you to get your daydreaming under control.

Whereas guilt relates to what we *did*, shame relates to who we *are*. And that's not so easy to change. We can modify bad behaviour, but we can't just become somebody different. So instead of changing, we hide. We hide the parts of ourselves that we think are bad or that we think other people will perceive as bad. And we end up pretending to be someone we're not. We sacrifice our authenticity in order to fit in. But as we're learning throughout this book, sacrificing authenticity is not a healthy thing to do.

Why it's important to overcome shame

Overcoming shame is crucial before you can overcome maladaptive daydreaming. Shame holds us back. It tells us we're not worth it. It tells us that no matter how much effort we make, we're never going to be good enough. Trying to do *anything* when you're overwhelmed with shame is almost impossible because shame urges you to hide rather than take action. Overcoming maladaptive daydreaming is not easy.

You don't need the added obstacle of trying to do it while wading through a muddy pool of shame.

In Chapter 8, we'll see how shame can drive maladaptive daydreaming. Shame tells you that you're not lovable or acceptable as you are. It says that in order to be loved and accepted, you need to become somebody else. And in your daydreams you can become someone else. Non-daydreamers can't get away from themselves, but we can. We can avoid our shame by creating a daydream version of ourselves who doesn't have any of our shameful characteristics.

But when we use daydreaming to escape from shame, we're making the problem worse. Shame hurts. And if the only way we can escape that pain is by daydreaming, we'll become dependent on our daydreams. It's only by getting rid of the shame that we will have any chance of overcoming maladaptive daydreaming, because while our daydreaming is our way of avoiding painful shame, we won't be able to give it up.

That's why it's so important that we learn to like ourselves. Once you like yourself – genuinely, deeply like yourself – shame can't survive. By the end of this chapter, you'll understand where your feelings of shame come from and you'll have learned some strategies to get rid of them.

Why daydreamers feel shame

In my experience, virtually all immersive and maladaptive daydreamers feel some level of shame about their daydreaming. But why? Where does that shame come from? There are two reasons daydreamers might be ashamed of their daydreaming: there is shame about the fact that we daydream, and then there is shame about what we daydream about.

SHAME ABOUT BEING A DAYDREAMER

We have a natural desire to be accepted by the people around us. Feeling that you're in some way different, even if that difference isn't inherently negative, puts distance between you and others. And in that distance lies the possibility of rejection. So it's natural to want to hide anything about yourself that makes you different. And when you feel you need to hide part of who you are, shame inevitably follows.

Researchers don't yet know how common immersive daydreaming is, but we can safely say most people don't experience vivid narrative daydreams. It's probably not that rare, but people don't tend to talk about their daydreaming. You've probably never met anyone who admitted to daydreaming in the way you do. And so it's natural to wonder if it's just you. And when you think you're the only person in your social circle who has these vivid narrative daydreams, it's natural to feel some level of shame about that.

WHAT SOCIETY CONSIDERS "NORMAL"

Our society can be unforgiving of some of the traits that are part of being an immersive or maladaptive daydreamer. We're told that imaginary friends are something you grow out of. So when your characters stay with you into adolescence and adulthood, you might worry that there's something wrong with you or that you'll be ridiculed if you admit to it. Behaviours such as pacing or talking out loud can look odd to non-daydreamers, so we naturally feel uncomfortable about being caught doing them. And there's an unspoken expectation that what we daydream about is supposed to be realistic. Have you ever worried about being mocked for daydreaming about something that couldn't possibly happen? In all those cases, it's not that there's something inherently wrong with you; it's that you have things going on in your head that non-daydreamers don't understand and are therefore likely to be a bit uncomfortable with.

Some of the judgements and assumptions you might have made about being a daydreamer come not from what's OK but from what society accepts as "normal". As a child, you were hypersensitive to the opinions of important people in your life – parents, teachers, siblings, friends. Hearing a parent say that "talking to yourself is the first sign of madness", for example, would have been worrying and upsetting. Having an older sibling laugh at you for pretending to be a superhero would have been embarrassing. And when things like that happen in childhood, especially if they generate unpleasant emotions, they stick in your memory and shape the beliefs you have about yourself. You start to become self-conscious about your daydreaming. You feel bad for doing it. You worry that there's something wrong with you. And that's how shame sets in. For many maladaptive daydreamers, shame starts young. And the younger it starts, the more ingrained it gets and the harder it will be to shift.

As you get older, you might develop further limiting beliefs that pile more shame on top of what's already there. You compare yourself to others. You see your friends getting on with their lives and achieving things, and you feel as though you're falling behind. You start to see yourself as a failure or a loser. That's your shame talking.

MYTHS ABOUT MALADAPTIVE DAYDREAMING

As more people have become aware of maladaptive daydreaming, especially while immersive daydreaming remains relatively unknown, myths about maladaptive daydreaming have started to circulate online. Maladaptive daydreaming is, correctly, often portrayed as a mental-health problem. But it's sometimes implied that it's the daydreaming, rather than the addiction to it, that causes all the suffering. Hopefully, by now, you understand that being a daydreamer isn't a bad thing *unless it interferes with other parts of your life.* The problem is that most of the non-daydreamers you know probably don't realize that. They may worry about you if they believe the myth that being a daydreamer automatically means you're mentally ill.

And, of course, there's still stigma attached to having *any* mental-health condition. Things are getting better as more people are talking openly about their mental health, but it's hard to talk openly about a condition that most people have never heard of.

If you're feeling some shame about being a daydreamer, that's normal. But it's not helpful.

SHAME ABOUT WHAT WE DAYDREAM ABOUT

In Chapter 3, I mentioned some of the common things that we daydream about and looked at why having dark or violent daydreams isn't automatically a cause for concern. But the content of our daydreams isn't a major part of this book. That's because it doesn't matter what you daydream about. Overcoming maladaptive daydreaming is about developing a positive relationship with your daydreaming and not letting it interfere with other aspects of your life. The content of your daydreams is your private business, and it's not for me or anyone else to tell you what is and is not OK in the safe space of your imagination.

That being said, there are ways of relating to the content of your daydreams that can lead to shame and are therefore unhelpful. In most cases, it's not the content of your daydreams that's the problem, but rather the judgements you're making about it.

SHAME ABOUT HAVING FEELINGS FOR YOUR CHARACTERS

We've spent years reassuring ourselves that we can tell the difference between fantasy and reality. But when we cling too tightly to the distinction between fantasy and reality, we can end up denying or judging the parts of our daydreams that *are* real. For example, we might tell ourselves that it's ridiculous to get emotionally attached to a character we made up. We think there's something wrong with having feelings for someone who doesn't exist. But most people have felt empathy for a character in a novel or cried over something that happened in a movie. Being emotionally attached to our daydream characters isn't fundamentally any different, except that if we've maintained the same plot for months or years, obviously the connection we feel will deepen over time. The idea that you shouldn't have real feelings about something you imagined is simply not true – but all too often we feel ashamed about doing exactly that.

SHAME ABOUT YOUR DAYDREAM SELF

Another way in which we judge the content of our daydreams is that we tell ourselves that our daydream self isn't real. We'll come back to this in more detail in Chapter 13, but for now let me reassure you that the person you become in the safe space of your imagination, free from societal expectations and the fear of rejection, is every bit as valid and real as the person you are in the real world. There's nothing wrong with wanting to be funny, or smart, or talented, or whatever attributes your daydream self has that your real-world self currently lacks.

The person you are now is not the person you're going to be for the rest of your life. People grow and change and develop. We acquire new skills, we change our mindset and we gain confidence, experience and the respect of others. Your daydream self can be a powerful guide to the kind of person you want to become, and there is nothing wrong with using your imagination to explore that.

Being a daydreamer doesn't make you a bad person

Your daydreaming will never go away, but neither does it have to define you. By now, I hope you can see that your ability to immersively daydream isn't the problem. Your ability to daydream, in and of itself, isn't harmful. It's not responsible for holding you back in life, although it can feel that way if you've been daydreaming for years and you're painfully aware of how much time you've wasted. It's the relationship you have with your daydreaming, and the way you're using it, that causes all the problems. And you can fix that.

As we saw in Chapter 3, your maladaptive daydreaming is not your fault. You didn't choose to become addicted to your thoughts. You didn't know how damaging your daydreaming was going to become or how hard it would be to break free of it. Daydreaming was your coping mechanism. It protected you. It kept you safe. And at some point, it got out of control and became maladaptive. Hopefully, you're beginning to understand why and you're beginning to see that it wasn't your fault.

When you can accept that your maladaptive daydreaming isn't your fault, you can let go of the idea that being a maladaptive daydreamer somehow makes you a bad person. It doesn't. It might mean some bad things happened to you, but having something bad happen to you and being a bad person are two different things. Bad things happen to good people.

When you understand that maladaptive daydreaming is an addiction and you appreciate just how hard it is to break an addiction to your own thoughts, you don't need to feel bad about the fact that you can't stop daydreaming. If you can't overcome maladaptive daydreaming on your own, using just willpower, that doesn't make you weak. It makes you human.

So if having maladaptive daydreaming doesn't make you a bad person and doesn't make you weak, could you start to believe that you're neither of those things? Could you start to let go of the shame you feel about being a daydreamer?

While you're making that mental adjustment, think about whether you've been blaming your daydreaming for everything that's going wrong in your life. When maladaptive daydreaming is stealing hours out of every day, it's easy to think you'd be happier and more successful if you stopped daydreaming. But it wasn't your daydreaming that originally made a mess of your life. Something else did that, and daydreaming was the method you used to cope with it. Are you blaming your daydreaming for problems that would have been there anyway? Because it's going to be a lot harder to make peace with your daydreaming if you're blaming it for problems it didn't cause.

How to overcome shame

Shame takes its power from secrecy. When we're ashamed of something, it's natural to want to hide it. We think that if people knew about our daydreaming, they'd judge us or reject us. So to avoid the pain that would involve, we keep quiet. We go to great lengths to make sure no one finds out about our daydreaming.

But that's exactly what shame wants us to do. Hiding our daydreaming feeds our shame. When we hide something that's a fundamental part of who we are, we're suppressing our authentic self.

We're constantly trying to be someone we're not. That takes a huge amount of mental effort. And it prevents us from deeply connecting with people, because we never allow anyone to see who we truly are. In the long term, it's damaging to our mental health. Keeping part of who you are a secret will eventually do more harm than the rejection you're trying to avoid.

You've probably guessed where I'm going with this. A crucial part of overcoming the shame you feel about being a daydreamer is admitting that you're a daydreamer. The antidote to shame is to stop hiding. And if that thought terrifies you because you've never told *anyone*, you're not alone. It's completely normal to feel you'd rather die than tell someone what goes on in your head.

There's a big difference between telling someone you're a daydreamer and telling them all the details of what you daydream about. The former is something you need to get used to doing. The latter is up to you. I've never told anyone what I daydream about in more than general terms. If you can't face telling anyone about your plot or your characters, you don't have to. But you do have to stop hiding the fact that you daydream.

START BY JOINING AN ONLINE SUPPORT GROUP

If you've never opened up to anyone about your daydreaming, a good place to start is online. There are many online groups dedicated to maladaptive daydreaming. You can find links to some of them in the Resources section. These groups give you a safe space where you can connect with other daydreamers and talk openly about how your daydreaming affects you. Most groups will allow you to post anonymously, and you have the added security of knowing you can leave the group if you don't feel comfortable there.

Joining an online support group will benefit you in three main ways in addition to helping you overcome your shame.

First, you'll see that you aren't alone. You'll meet other people who have movies playing in their heads all the time, who pace around in circles listening to music and who fall in love with people who don't exist. When you've spent your whole life thinking you're the only one, that can be incredibly validating.

Second, you'll have a safe space where you can be your authentic self without fear of judgement or rejection. When you have somewhere you can practise being authentically you, you'll see that you're not such a bad person after all. It can be the first step in learning to like yourself.

Third, you'll meet other people who are working to overcome their maladaptive daydreaming, and you can share tips and support each other. Almost no one overcomes *any* addiction on their own. It helps to know that there are other people facing the same challenges and that you're all in this together.

TALKING TO FRIENDS AND FAMILY

Once you're comfortable connecting with other daydreamers online, the next step is to start opening up to people in real life. This will feel scary. You'll be aware that once you've told someone, you can't take what you've shared back. You'll worry about how they'll react. The risk of being judged or ridiculed is real. But it's important you try. Daydreaming is a fundamental part of who you are. If you're hiding it from someone, you're not being authentic around them. You may worry that admitting you're a daydreamer will damage your relationship, but in the long term, so will keeping secrets.

One of the problems with talking to your friends and family, though, is that most of them won't know what maladaptive daydreaming is. It's likely you'll have to explain it to every person you tell. And even when you get comfortable with it, that will be frustrating. If someone says "I'm sorry I act impulsively at times; it's because I have ADHD", that can be all the explanation that's needed. But saying "I'm sorry I seem distracted at times; I'm struggling with maladaptive daydreaming" isn't likely to end the conversation. You'll need to explain what it is. You don't have to say what you daydream about, but it can be helpful to say that you have a plot and characters so that people understand this isn't what they mean by "daydreaming" and it isn't something you can just decide to stop doing.

Although I recommend being as open as you can with people, you don't have to tell everyone. Start with the people you trust not to judge you. People who love you will accept you regardless of what goes on in your head. Remember, you haven't changed. You're still the person they met and liked. You're just being more authentically you, and a true friend will appreciate that.

There may be people in your life that you choose not to tell. If someone is judgemental about mental illness or thinks addiction is a "choice", they may not be accepting of your daydreaming. That can be hard if it's someone close to you, such as a family member. But it's their problem, not yours. If you know someone well enough to know that they won't accept your daydreaming or support you in your recovery, then it's perfectly OK not to tell them. Remember, your goal here is to reduce the shame you feel about being a daydreamer. If someone is likely to think your daydreaming is something you *should* be ashamed of, it's probably better not to discuss it with them.

Challenging the negative beliefs you have about your daydreaming

The shame you feel about being a daydreamer will block you from developing a healthier relationship with your daydreaming. Now that you understand the difference between immersive daydreaming and maladaptive daydreaming, you can let go of the idea that being a daydreamer is inherently a bad thing. It's only the maladaptive part that's a problem. Many immersive daydreamers live happy, successful, fulfilled lives. But even once you can see that the shame you feel is misplaced, it isn't always that easy to let go of.

It helps to identify specifically why you believe it's so bad to be a daydreamer. These beliefs may have crept into your subconscious a long time ago without you giving them much conscious thought. It's only when you bring them into conscious awareness and examine them critically that you can see they don't make sense. That's the first step in letting them go.

Let's examine some of the common beliefs that feed the shame we feel about our daydreaming.

I DAYDREAM ALL THE TIME; I NEVER GET ANYTHING DONE

When your daydreaming is out of control, you spend a *lot* of time lost in your fantasies. And that means a lot of time *not* working on real life. So a lot of things don't get done. And it's easy to blame your daydreaming for the negative consequences of that. But, fundamentally, it's not a daydreaming problem, it's a time-management problem.

Many of the negative consequences of daydreaming come from prioritizing daydreaming over something more important. It was what you *didn't* do that got you into trouble. You procrastinated. Everyone does that at some point. Everyone occasionally chooses something that's fun in the moment over something that's more important in the long term. Doing that doesn't make you a failure; it makes you human. And you probably had a lot more fun daydreaming than your non-daydreamer friend did mindlessly scrolling through social media.

I'M EMBARRASSED ABOUT THE CONTENT OF MY DAYDREAMS

Judging the content of your daydreams can lead to a lot of unnecessary shame. It doesn't matter what goes on in the private space of your imagination. Nothing should be off limits. No one else is going to know what happens in your daydream world unless you choose to tell them. The only person who has to approve of the content of your daydreams is you.

It's easy to assume that what happens in your daydream world is a reflection of your innermost wishes and desires. So if bad things happen in your daydreams, you might wonder if you secretly want those things in real life. But sometimes a good story is just a good story. If nothing bad ever happened in your daydreams, you wouldn't have a plot. What happens in your daydream world doesn't say anything about who you are in the real world.

DAYDREAMING ABOUT REAL PEOPLE FEELS CREEPY

It's common to base daydream characters on people you know (or know of) in real life. And it can then be embarrassing interacting with that person, especially if your character has been doing things you know the real person wouldn't do. You might wonder if it's OK to base a character on a real person or whether it's OK to edit that character so that they think and act in ways the real person wouldn't.

But, as we saw in Chapter 1, you can't put a real person in your daydreams. As soon as you start daydreaming about someone you know, you create a character that's based on them. The real person goes on living their own life. Your character evolves in whatever way you want. They can stay close to the real person, or they can evolve away from them. You can edit them a little bit or you can edit them a lot. It doesn't matter. You've created a daydream character that no one else ever needs to know about. There's nothing wrong with using a real person as inspiration in that process.

IT'S NARCISSISTIC TO DAYDREAM ABOUT BEING A BETTER VERSION OF MYSELF

It's common to daydream as an idealized version of yourself. Your daydream self might be smarter, funnier or more confident than your real-world self. And sometimes we think there's something wrong with that. We feel awkward about pretending to be someone we're not.

In Chapter 13, we'll look at whether becoming an idealized version of yourself in your daydreams really is pretending to be someone you're not. In many cases, you're giving yourself the freedom to be you. It's not your daydream self that's idealized so much as the environment you're putting them into. No matter what happens in your daydreams – even if the setting feels far from idealized – your daydream self has one advantage you don't. They can't fail. You're always in control of the outcome. Wouldn't you be more confident in real life if you knew you couldn't fail?

Becoming an idealized version of yourself in your daydreams isn't about deluding yourself that you're someone you're not. It's about exploring what you could be if you weren't constrained by real-world limitations and uncertainties. That's a useful thing to explore.

Sola's story

When I spoke to Sola about how she overcame maladaptive daydreaming, she identified releasing shame and embracing self-love as crucial parts of the process.

"If I could summarize the process in one sentence, it was getting comfortable with being myself. That was the core. The reason why I had to fall into my daydreams was because there were parts of me I wasn't accepting.

"One of the key things was to keep digging into my curiosity. I would keep trying to learn about myself, and also through my real-life situation I would get to know myself. I think when you have that awareness and when you have real-life situations, you kind of grow. I also remember that whenever I was in any social situation, I would always journal that down: how I felt and what triggered me, and what that reminded me of. I also remember having a lot of emotions that I wasn't able to feel before. I had been very repressive. I was trying to be a nice girl. I wasn't very familiar with the emotion of rage or being furious or being assertive and setting boundaries. Those things were just not in my dictionary, and that is something that I slowly learned as I faced new situations.

"I think if you're a daydreamer, you know the potential you have inside. Because you have so many weird daydreams. I thought they were telling me something, but they were just being troublesome. I remember being curious about very deep questions like who am I, and what am I supposed to do in this world? I think daydreamers can have really big dreams in their head, and intuitively they know what they are meant to do. I think that's what led me to keep digging into myself."

Sola's experience shows how overcoming maladaptive daydreaming involves so much more than just focussing on the daydreaming itself. Sola had to reconnect with her authentic self in order to build a real life that she enjoys more than her daydreams. And that all began with releasing the shame that made her uncomfortable about being herself.

Beyond shame – learning to like yourself

Shame tells you that you're a bad person, so if you can learn to like yourself, the shame will fall away. I'm going to give you a couple of tools that can help you get started on that process.

LOOK IN THE MIRROR

The first one is simple. You have to get comfortable with looking at yourself in the mirror. Many daydreamers don't like seeing their own reflection. That's understandable. If you spend a lot of time being someone else in your head, it can be disconcerting to be confronted with the proof that you aren't that person in real life. Even if your daydream self is closely based on your real-world self, you've probably still made a few improvements to your appearance. When you look in the mirror, you compare your flawed real-world self with your idealized daydream self, and that can immediately make you feel bad about yourself and trigger shame.

So I want you to look at yourself in the mirror. Really look at yourself. If you can, smile. See how it makes your face light up. Get comfortable with your reflection.

If this is difficult, and it probably will be at first, you can try this exercise. Look at yourself in the mirror. Now imagine that you are your daydream self, standing face-to-face with the real-world self you see in the mirror. With compassion, thank your real-world self for creating you. Thank your real-world self for the awesome life they have given you and for all the good things that have happened in the daydream world. And then, when you've connected with the gratitude you feel toward your real-world self, ask them how their life is going. Let this evolve into a conversation between your daydream self and your real-world self. Let your daydream self advise your real-world self about how to handle any difficulties they may be facing.

If this feels weird, think about it this way. If you're anything like me, your daydream self is the most amazing, talented, inspirational person you know. They can do anything. Wouldn't you love to have someone like that on your side in real life? Well, you do. You carry them inside your head. They're with you in every single moment. You can tap into that. You and your awesome daydream self can form a partnership to take on the world – your real world. How empowering is that?

Talking to yourself in the mirror as your daydream self might feel silly at first. But keep trying. Being comfortable looking at your reflection will help you to overcome your shame.

SEE YOUR SHAME AS A SEPARATE CHARACTER

It can be helpful to distance yourself from your shame by seeing it as an entity separate from you. A CBT counsellor once encouraged me to see my shame as the "parrot on my shoulder". I could then challenge shameful thoughts by arguing with the parrot.

Daydreamers can do better than this. Our characters are much more real to us than an imaginary parrot on the shoulder. You can nominate or create a character that embodies your shame. A character who is always trying to hold you back, keep you invisible, make you play small. Whenever you catch yourself feeling ashamed, imagine that your "shame character" is the one telling you how much of a failure you are. And then you tell them, firmly, why they're wrong. If you need to, become your awesome daydream self for a minute and tell your bullying shame character where to go.

The reason this works is that it allows you to think of your shame thoughts as if they're coming from someone else. You can acknowledge the feeling of shame without identifying with it. You can say to yourself *"Oh, that's my shame character showing up again."* And that little bit of distance gives you an opportunity to challenge the feeling. You can choose whether to believe what your shame character is saying to you. You can choose to argue with them. Or, if you want, you can tell them to get lost. Whatever helps you move past the shameful feeling.

THERE'S NO SHAME IN ASKING FOR HELP

If your shame is deep-rooted and the things you've learned in this chapter aren't helping you to shift it, it might be something you need to explore with a trained counsellor. Many of the beliefs we have about ourselves formed when we were young, and it can take a lot of work to unpick them. For some people it's too much to do alone. That doesn't make you weak – it just means a lot of difficult and complicated things happened to you. A good therapist can help you make sense of that. I hope this chapter has shown you why it's so important that you reach out for help if you need it. Because once you let go of your shame and learn to like yourself, everything else in life, including overcoming your maladaptive daydreaming, will be that much easier.

Two things to do right now

To end this chapter, there are two things I would like you to do right now, in addition to downloading and completing the accompanying worksheet.

JOIN A SUPPORT GROUP

Research online maladaptive daydreaming support groups and join at least one. Post an introduction about yourself. Try to comment on at least three other posts. Set a reminder for yourself to check in with the group at least a couple of times a week, and try to post or comment each time you do.

TELL SOMEONE ABOUT YOUR DAYDREAMING

Who do you hide your daydreaming from? Whose support would you like to have as you work to overcome your maladaptive daydreaming? Who can you trust to accept you without judgement?

Pick one friend or family member to tell about your daydreaming. You could send them an article or video about maladaptive daydreaming. You could even show them this book. And if you're not sure how to start the conversation, you could say something like "I've realized that I have a mental-health problem called maladaptive daydreaming. I'm trying to overcome it, but it's not easy. I'm telling you because I trust you not to judge me and because it would mean a lot to me to have your support."

If you choose who to tell carefully and let them know how they can support you, the conversation will probably go better than you expect. And it will be a relief to have one person that you don't have to hide your daydreaming from. Good luck!

Worksheet: Why are you ashamed of your daydreaming?

The worksheet that accompanies this chapter will help you discover the specific beliefs that are driving your shame so that you can start to challenge and overcome those beliefs.

Download the worksheet at:
https://daydreamplace.com/extreme-imagination/worksheet-chapter7.pdf

CHAPTER 8

UNDERSTANDING WHY YOU ESCAPE

As we saw in Chapter 4, your maladaptive daydreaming is probably causing problems in every area of your life. So if your daydreaming is doing so much harm, why can't you just stop? What is it that draws you back into your daydream world over and over again even when you know it's not good for you?

The answer is simple. On some level it *is* good for you. Few things in life are either 100% good or 100% bad, and daydreaming is no exception. In order to overcome your maladaptive daydreaming, you'll need to understand what it's doing for you. Your daydreaming is giving you something, otherwise it wouldn't be hard to stop. Once you understand what need your daydreaming is meeting, you'll have to figure out how to meet that need from a combination of immersive daydreaming and living in reality.

Daydreaming feels great while you're doing it

As we saw in Chapter 2, one feature of an addictive behaviour is that it's something in which the individual "finds temporary relief or pleasure". Many addictive behaviours are addictive precisely because they're enjoyable. They feel good in the moment. And afterwards, you remember how good it felt, so you want to do it again. No matter how much harm your maladaptive daydreaming is causing, no matter how determined you are to stop doing it, nothing beats that feeling of relaxing into your daydream world. Daydreaming is fun. And so there will be a part of you that doesn't want to give it up, because why would you want to give up something you enjoy?

But, as we saw in Chapter 6, you won't be giving up completely. Turning your maladaptive daydreaming into immersive daydreaming puts you back in control. It sets you free to enjoy your daydreams without any of the harmful side effects. So the fact that daydreaming is enjoyable isn't a problem.

Daydreaming as a coping mechanism

Daydreaming becomes maladaptive when you use it as an unhealthy coping mechanism. A coping mechanism is anything you do to help you manage the negative emotions connected with some problem in your life. And a coping mechanism is unhealthy if it allows you to escape from the problem but does nothing to solve it. That's what maladaptive daydreaming does: when you snap back to reality, the problem is still there, urging you to escape again.

If you're a maladaptive daydreamer, it's probably because something in real life isn't the way you want it to be. That could be either because there's something going on in your life that shouldn't be or because something isn't going on that should be.

We'll look in more detail at what you might be coping with in a minute. But I want to emphasize that if you're using your daydreaming as a coping mechanism, you won't be able to overcome your maladaptive daydreaming until you have either solved the problem or found an alternative (and preferably healthier) way to cope with it. If you're dealing with memories of a past trauma, you might need a therapist or support group to help you process it. If you're coping with mental or physical health problems, you'll need to work with your doctor to manage those. And if your daydreaming is providing something that real life isn't, you'll have to get that thing in real life before you'll be able to overcome your maladaptive daydreaming.

DO YOU *NEED* A COPING MECHANISM?

You have to be honest with yourself about whether this is the right time for you to be trying to overcome your maladaptive daydreaming. If you're going through an unusually stressful time, you might need your daydreaming to get you through it. And if your daydreaming is the only way you can cope with something that's out of your control, it might not be safe for you to stop. You might end up swapping your maladaptive daydreaming for an even more dangerous addiction.

If you have any doubts about whether it's safe for you to reduce your daydreaming, or if the thought of spending more time in reality terrifies you, I urge you to talk to a qualified mental-health professional about your situation. They can help you find healthier ways to manage the problem your daydreaming is enabling you to escape from.

WHAT IF YOU DON'T KNOW WHAT YOU'RE COPING WITH?

How can you tackle the thing you're trying to avoid if you don't know what it is? That can happen. As you learned from Mia's story in Chapter 5, daydreaming to escape from uncomfortable thoughts can become so automatic that you don't even consciously recognize that the uncomfortable thoughts are there. You just suddenly find yourself daydreaming without understanding why.

If that's the case for you, you may need to do some detective work. One option is to ask yourself when your daydreaming first became maladaptive. This is not the same as trying to remember when you first daydreamed. That probably happened when you were very young. But when do you first remember your daydreaming being a problem? When did you realize you couldn't control it? If you can pinpoint the time when your daydreaming first became maladaptive, and you can remember what was going on in your life at that time, that might help you understand what you're running away from.

It's common to feel sad, lonely or ashamed when you come out of a daydream and back to the real world. Tuning into these feelings can also help you understand what you're escaping from. Next time coming back to reality is painful, ask yourself which is worse – leaving your perfect daydream world or returning to the imperfect reality? If it's leaving the daydream that's hard, then your daydreaming might be meeting a need that isn't being met in real life. If it's returning to reality that's the problem, that suggests your daydreaming is providing an escape from something that's wrong with real life.

The content of your daydreams might also indicate what you're escaping from. What's the main difference in how you *feel* when you're in your daydream world versus when you're in reality? Is your daydream world giving you a feeling of safety? Of excitement? Of being loved? Of being accepted? It's better to look at the emotions rather than the events. *What* you daydream about might be inspired by things you've watched or read, but the emotions you *feel* in the daydream are usually the emotions your subconscious needs you to experience. Your subconscious speaks to you through emotions, so don't take your daydreams too literally.

Remember, taking any emotion or situation to the extreme is usually unhealthy. So if life is giving you too much of one thing, your daydreaming might give you the opposite to restore balance. That doesn't mean you don't need the thing that real life is already giving you. For example, if you have a boring but secure job, your daydreams might be full of excitement and unpredictability. That doesn't mean that security and safety aren't important to you; it just means that life is already meeting that need. But you *also* have a need for interest and novelty. And if that need isn't being met in real life, it will come out in your daydreams. It doesn't mean you want life to be as wild and dangerous as it is in your daydreams; it just means that currently you don't have the right balance of security and excitement.

It's important to understand what your daydreaming is doing for you, because if you understand why you daydream, you know what to work on so that you won't need to daydream as much. More importantly, understanding what you're getting from daydreaming will help you to stop seeing your daydreaming as the enemy. Your daydreaming is your mind's way of taking care of you. It might not be working. It might be causing a whole lot of other problems. But your daydreaming isn't out to get you. It's trying, in its own misguided way, to help you.

What need might your daydreaming be meeting?

When real life isn't providing everything you need to stay mentally healthy, your mind will try to supply what's missing. But for immersive and maladaptive daydreamers, this works a bit too well. Our minds can create something so vividly that, even though we know it's fantasy, we have a real emotional response to it. We really can meet our emotional needs through daydreaming.

If your daydreaming is meeting a need that isn't being met any other way, you won't be able to overcome your maladaptive daydreaming no matter how hard you try. If you *need* to daydream because something vital will be missing from your life if you don't, then the daydreaming is in control. You have to meet that need in real life so you don't need to find it in your daydreams.

Let's look at some of the needs our daydreaming might be meeting.

A NEED FOR CONNECTION

Our daydream characters know everything about us. We can be completely honest and vulnerable with them. We can be our authentic selves without fear of judgement or rejection. We develop deep and intimate connections because nothing is hidden.

But in the real world, we struggle. We neglect our real-life friendships in favour of our daydream friendships. And we hide our daydreaming. Many of us even hide who we are. We never give people a chance to truly know us. And that means we don't develop the deep connections we're craving.

A NEED FOR AUTHENTICITY

We all want to feel safe being our authentic selves. But too many of us learned early in life that we weren't always unconditionally accepted for who we were. We learned that we had to sacrifice our authenticity if we wanted to fit in. But sacrificing your authenticity – pretending to be someone you're not – doesn't feel good. You long to be yourself. And the one place it is safe to be totally, unapologetically, authentically you is in your daydreams.

A NEED TO PROCESS AN EMOTION

Society teaches us that certain emotions aren't OK. For example, if you were punished as a child for something you did because you were angry, you got the message that expressing anger is bad. But we feel anger for a reason – usually because our boundaries have been violated. Anger is a signal that we need to assert ourselves.

All our emotions serve a purpose. When we try to ignore or repress them, they don't just go away. Repressed emotions can damage our mental, and even physical, health. But often it doesn't feel safe or appropriate to express an emotion in the real world. And that's where our daydreams come in. They give us an opportunity to work through difficult emotions in a safe space without fearing the consequences.

A NEED TO BE LOVED

We all want to be liked, appreciated and validated. We all want to feel that we matter to the people around us. But unfortunately, real life doesn't always meet that need. If you grew up in a family where your caregivers were always working or focussed on their own problems, it might have felt as though you didn't matter. It might have felt as if no one cared about you. So you might have turned to daydreaming to meet that natural human need.

A NEED TO FEEL SAFE

Safety is another basic human need. If you don't feel safe, either physically or emotionally, your natural reaction is to escape to somewhere you do feel safe. And perhaps the only place that feels safe is your daydream world.

A NEED TO FEEL IN CONTROL

Real life is unpredictable. Situations don't always turn out the way you want them to. And that can be frustrating, especially if you feel powerless to improve your situation because your circumstances are determined by forces outside your control. Your daydream world might be the only place where things work out the way *you* want them to.

A NEED TO EXPLORE

If most of your days follow a predictable pattern, real life may not be exciting or varied enough for you. You might be naturally curious. You might want to explore possibilities that simply don't exist in reality. You might want to explore what it would be like to live in another country or a different period of history. You might want to explore a world where magic is real.

This is a common need when real life is mundane and predictable and doesn't offer up much in the way of surprises or new experiences. It's not unusual for daydreamers to crave a level of novelty and excitement that real life simply can't keep up with.

YOUR NEEDS ARE VALID

The important point here is that you're not wrong, or selfish, for wanting any of these things. And it's not your fault that real life isn't providing them. Your daydreaming is not trying to damage your reality. It's trying to make up for the fact that your reality is not what you need it to be.

What is your daydreaming allowing you to escape from?

We've looked at how your daydreaming might be meeting a need. Now let's look at how your daydreaming might allow you to escape from something in real life.

When you use daydreaming to escape, what you're escaping from is typically some sort of emotional pain. Usually, it's not the situation itself that triggers your daydreaming; it's how you feel about the situation. And it's the fact that you don't want to continue feeling those feelings, and the only way you know how to get away from them is by daydreaming.

The problem is that the negative emotions don't necessarily go away when the bad situation passes. Even when you're no longer dealing with the stressful situation, the memory of it remains. And that memory can bring back the original emotions. Your maladaptive daydreaming might be the way you escape from something painful that's happening now. But it can also be how you avoid painful memories of something that happened a long time ago.

We use our daydreaming to escape because we never learned any other way to deal with negative emotions. Perhaps you grew up in an environment where negative emotions weren't acknowledged or taken seriously. Perhaps you were too young to understand that those negative emotions were signals that something was wrong. Or perhaps you suspected something was wrong but you were powerless to change it. All you knew was that you didn't like the way you were feeling. And so when you discovered that you could feel better by daydreaming, you adopted it as your coping mechanism. It was probably the only coping mechanism you had.

In Chapter 10, we'll look at healthier ways to deal with negative emotions so that you can be less dependent on daydreaming for emotional regulation. But first, let's look at some of the negative emotions you might be using your daydreaming to escape from.

TRAUMA

As we saw in Chapter 3, trauma is often the thing that caused your daydreaming to become maladaptive in the first place. Something happened that was overwhelming or too upsetting to face, so you ran away from it by daydreaming. And for as long as reality wasn't a nice place to be, you kept running. But trauma doesn't go away easily. Even if you aren't in the traumatic situation now, the memories of what happened to you might still be upsetting enough to push you into a daydream. And that means that whenever something happens that reminds you of the trauma, it will probably trigger your daydreaming.

SHAME

Shame is a powerful daydreaming trigger. It's one of the most uncomfortable of all emotions. So most of us will do almost anything to avoid feeling it. Shame can be overwhelming because when you think there's something fundamentally wrong with you, you're likely to think that feeling will never go away. But as we saw in Chapter 7, there *are* healthy ways that you can manage, and even overcome, your shame.

ANXIETY

Anxiety usually shows up as the fear of something happening, or even just the discomfort of not knowing what's going to happen. In real life, we can't always control what happens to us. But in our daydreams we can. And when we're used to controlling everything in our daydreams, the lack of control and predictability in real life can be terrifying.

But anxiety serves a purpose. It prompts us to plan for possible outcomes. What anxiety is urging us to do is to think through what's likely to happen and rehearse how we're going to deal with it. When we escape our anxiety by daydreaming, we don't prepare for the future, and so situations tend to take us by surprise and we handle them badly. And then we feel bad about how we reacted, and we escape from that bad feeling by daydreaming. So anxiety and daydreaming can feed on each other.

BOREDOM

Gabor Maté has described boredom as one of the least tolerable mental states (2018). I'd agree with that. Boredom is a powerful daydreaming trigger for me.

There are times when boredom might be a sign that it's OK to daydream. If you're stuck in traffic, for example, there might genuinely be nothing productive you can do in that moment, and if daydreaming makes the delay more tolerable, there's nothing wrong with that. But you need to be careful. I've often told myself I'm bored when what I mean is that the things I'm supposed to be doing are boring. In other words, I tell myself I'm bored when I'm actually procrastinating.

MENTAL EFFORT

Many daydreamers dislike tasks that require sustained focus or mental effort. And we use daydreaming to avoid those tasks. In the moment, daydreaming feels easier and more appealing than the task we should be focussing on.

DISSATISFACTION WITH REAL LIFE

Regardless of what you're using your daydreaming to escape from, when you're in your daydream world, you aren't working on real life. And when you ignore real life over a long time, it doesn't just stay the same; it gets worse. Friends drift away. Work suffers. You compare yourself to the people around you, and you see them making progress while you're not. And the worse you feel about the direction your life is taking, the more that feeling drives you into daydreaming. After a while, the stress of living a life that isn't the way you want it to be can be as powerful a daydreaming trigger as whatever you were originally escaping from.

The importance of tolerating negative emotions

With all of the emotions listed above, there's a threshold. You can tolerate a little bit of boredom, anxiety or mental challenge, but when it becomes too much you feel an urge to escape into a daydream. That concept of "too much" is something you can work with. When you're under a lot of stress, it takes only a little bit extra to tip you over into too much.

The negative emotions associated with too much stress can be powerful daydreaming triggers because most of us never learned to tolerate them. We learned early on that we could escape from negative emotions by daydreaming, so we never saw any reason to get used to feeling them. But escaping from a negative emotion doesn't make it go away. It might feel as if it's gone away while you're in the daydream, but all you've done is suppress it. As soon as you stop daydreaming, it's going to pop right back up again.

Here's an interesting thing. Emotions, on their own, last for an average of 90 seconds. That's right, 90 *seconds*. The reason most of us feel emotions for much longer than that is that we reinforce them with our thoughts. You don't need to daydream for hours to escape a negative emotion. You just need to be able to sit with it for a few minutes and wait for it to pass. We'll come back to how you can do that in Chapter 9.

I'm not saying the underlying reason for the emotion will pass in 90 seconds. It won't. If you're dealing with trauma or chronic shame, or if your life is constantly stressful or upsetting, negative emotions are going to keep popping up until you deal with the underlying issue. Escaping from the issue by daydreaming, or, worse, blaming your daydreaming for your problems as a way of avoiding the issue doesn't make the issue go away.

That's why it's so important not to try to overcome your maladaptive daydreaming in isolation. If daydreaming is the way you escape the pain associated with an unresolved problem, stopping daydreaming means you have to feel that pain again. And if daydreaming is the only coping mechanism you have, that pain will drive you straight back into daydreaming.

That's why it's imperative that *before* you try to take control of your daydreaming, you understand what daydreaming is protecting you from and make sure that you have a healthier strategy in place to manage it.

Therapy to process trauma

If you've realized that you're using your daydreaming to escape from something overwhelmingly painful, you might be scared about giving up your coping mechanism. But don't worry. There are ways you can work through your trauma so that instead of it being something you need to escape from, it becomes something you can face up to, deal with and move on from. Not everyone can do this on their own. Many of us need to work through our trauma with the support of a qualified therapist. But for maladaptive daydreamers, the thought of seeing a therapist can be terrifying. What if they haven't heard of maladaptive daydreaming? What if they don't take it seriously? And worst of all, what if they need to know what we daydream about?

Let's address those concerns by looking at what happens when you work with a therapist.

First of all, it's important to acknowledge that therapy isn't for everyone. If your trauma relates to an ongoing situation, you need to resolve the situation or remove yourself from it. All the therapy in the world isn't going to help you if you're constantly being re-traumatized. If that's your reality, then for as long as the situation persists, you'll probably need a coping mechanism. And that coping mechanism might be daydreaming. If you're trapped in ongoing traumatic circumstances, this might not be the right time to try to overcome maladaptive daydreaming. Your energy might be better directed at trying to resolve the situation that's driving your daydreaming.

It's also important to recognize that in many parts of the world therapy is expensive and waiting lists are long. Finding a compassionate, qualified therapist can be a challenge. If you can't access therapy for whatever reason, don't worry. The strategies in this book can still help you take control of your daydreaming. The process might just take more time, effort and commitment if you're doing it without professional support.

CHOOSING A THERAPY AND FINDING A THERAPIST

If therapy is an option for you, there are some things you should consider before reaching out to a therapist. Don't worry about finding a therapist who's familiar with maladaptive daydreaming. It isn't as important as you think. The purpose of therapy is to help you resolve the underlying trauma that you're using your daydreaming to escape from. If you know what you're escaping from, find a therapist who specializes in that. Once you're comfortable with them, you can tell them as much about your daydreaming as you feel they need to know – it won't be the main focus of your sessions.

Therapy can be either skills-based, where you learn specific skills and techniques to manage life's challenges, or person-centred, where you talk to a therapist about your personal situation. The main skills-based therapies are CBT and DBT.

CBT has been scientifically shown to be effective in managing a range of mental-health problems. It teaches you to notice and challenge unhelpful thinking patterns, such as excessive worry or rumination. At the time of writing, CBT is the only skills-based therapy that has been shown to be helpful in treating maladaptive daydreaming.

Whereas CBT focusses on managing your *thoughts*, DBT helps you to manage your *emotions*. If you're emotionally dysregulated – in other words, if you find it difficult or impossible to control your emotions or if negative emotions feel intolerable to you – then DBT might be a better starting point than CBT. If you've been using daydreaming to escape from negative emotions since you were a child, you probably never learned healthier ways of managing your feelings. DBT can help with that. Both CBT and DBT teach you to manage uncomfortable thoughts and feelings instead of escaping from them and are, therefore, healthy coping mechanisms.

MY EXPERIENCE OF DBT

I never learned healthy ways to regulate my emotions. I discovered at a young age that I could run away from distressing emotions by daydreaming. And for most of my life that was the *only* way I could manage negative emotions.

But the belief I developed from constantly running away from my emotions was that emotions can't be controlled. They just come and go, and there's nothing you can do about it. That had always been my experience. And even when I did CBT, no one told me differently. CBT taught me that I should challenge unhelpful thoughts, but none of my CBT therapists ever mentioned challenging unhelpful emotions.

It was when I was admitted to hospital following a breakdown that I was introduced to DBT and to the idea that emotional regulation is a skill that can be learned. It was a revelation. So much so that I signed up to do six months of DBT as an outpatient. It changed my life.

Once I learned techniques to manage my emotions, I wasn't dependent on my daydreaming as my only means of emotional regulation. It had been meeting a need for me, and now I had the skills to meet that need in a healthier way. And that made it much easier to control my daydreaming, because it had become something I could choose to do rather than something I needed to do.

WHAT TYPE OF THERAPY IS RIGHT FOR YOU?

In both CBT and DBT you learn skills, so there's less emphasis on your situation and challenges. Therefore, CBT and DBT are often taught in group settings. And, importantly for maladaptive daydreamers, they can be successfully mastered without you ever needing to tell your therapist about your daydreaming.

In contrast, counselling – or person-centred therapy – involves working one-to-one with a therapist. Instead of learning a defined set of skills, you can set the agenda. You choose what you want to work on.

You could choose to see a counsellor specifically to work on your maladaptive daydreaming. However, if you know what you're using your daydreaming to escape from, it might be better to ask a counsellor to help you with the underlying issue. I've been going to counselling for several years to help me manage my depression, and as my depression has improved, I've found it easier to control my daydreaming. My therapist knows about my daydreaming, but it isn't the focus of our sessions and we rarely discuss it.

Alternatively, if you aren't sure what's driving your maladaptive daydreaming, a skilful therapist should be able to help you figure it out.

Don't worry if your therapist doesn't know anything about maladaptive daydreaming. If they can help you identify and address the underlying issue, you'll be in a much better place to take control of your daydreaming. Also, maladaptive daydreaming has many things in common with other behavioural addictions, so any therapist with experience in helping people overcome addiction should be able to support you in overcoming maladaptive daydreaming.

JENNA'S EXPERIENCE OF COUNSELLING

Like most maladaptive daydreamers, Jenna found it hard to talk about her daydreaming, even in therapy. Most of us have kept our daydreaming a secret for so long that it feels uncomfortable bringing it out into the open, even in the safe, confidential environment of therapy. If you're seeking therapy for an underlying issue, you may decide not to tell your therapist about your daydreaming until you feel comfortable with them. But your therapist can help you better if you're not hiding anything.

As Jenna explained: "I finally decided to be really fully honest with her the last time I went in. Because I realized, if I'm not being super honest with her about everything, then what's the point? But it's such a weird thing to do. I felt like a freak."

"Did she understand what you were describing?" I asked her.

"I think so. I know to her it's very interesting. Because she's never dealt with anybody that has this. So she asks lots of questions."

"And how did you feel during the session? Was it comfortable talking to her?"

"No! In the session I was pretty keyed up. And she knew I was. I was very twitchy and nervous. Your daydream world is something you don't share with anybody else ever. It's probably the most personal private part of me. So it's very hard to tell somebody much about it. Especially if you don't know if they're going to judge you. But then afterwards I was like, OK, she didn't seem to judge me, and I felt glad that I did it."

As we saw in Chapter 7, telling people about your daydreaming is one of the ways you can lessen the shame you feel about it. And therapy is one of the safest environments in which to open up. Everything you say is confidential, and the therapist won't judge you.

In any type of therapy, you shouldn't have to discuss what you daydream about unless you want to. It's not relevant. The important thing to address is how your daydreaming is affecting you. If you're using it as an unhealthy coping mechanism, you'll need to learn healthier ways of coping. That can be done without ever going into detail about the contents of your daydreams.

Therapy isn't accessible to everyone. But if it's an option for you, I'd urge you to seriously consider it. As we saw in Chapter 6, you have to take responsibility for your own healing. But that doesn't mean you have to do everything on your own. Sometimes, taking responsibility means accepting that you need support. And a qualified therapist can support you in your journey to overcoming maladaptive daydreaming, even if they don't know what it's like to be a daydreamer.

Worksheet: What need is your daydreaming meeting?

The worksheet that accompanies this chapter will help you to understand what problem your mind was attempting to solve by maladaptively daydreaming. You'll also evaluate the pros and cons of overcoming your maladaptive daydreaming.

Download the worksheet at:
https://daydreamplace.com/extreme-imagination/worksheet-chapter8.pdf

CHAPTER 9

MAKING REAL LIFE WORTH COMING BACK TO

Before you can overcome maladaptive daydreaming, you have to make real life somewhere you want to be. Your daydream world is fun, exciting and safe; you can be who you want to be and achieve what you want to achieve. If real life can't compare to that, how are you ever going to be able to reduce your daydreaming? Why would you want to swap your perfect imaginary life for a dreary, boring and quite possibly painful reality?

Part of you knows you need to develop a healthier relationship with your daydreaming. You know your imaginary world is taking over, and it's damaging other areas of your life. But as we've seen, your daydreaming is how you escape from a real life you don't want to be in. Your ability to immersively daydream isn't going to go away. Your daydream world will always be just a thought away. If you're going to develop a healthier relationship with your daydreaming, you *have* to make your real life somewhere you want to be.

You maladaptively daydream because your life is a mess

Many daydreamers find their mood crashes after a long daydream. When you come back to reality, you realize that your life is still just as much of a mess as it was when you dived into your daydream to get away from it. But now, after daydreaming, you're even more aware of the huge gap between the life you're daydreaming about and the life you're living. And that gap feels overwhelming.

When coming back to reality feels painful, that's your mind's way of telling you that real life isn't giving you everything you need. That's why your daydreaming became maladaptive. And, as we saw in Chapter 4, being a maladaptive daydreamer can itself mess up your life in lots of different ways. So if you've been a maladaptive daydreamer for a while, it would be surprising if your life wasn't a mess. But that's not a situation you have to accept. It's a situation you can do something about.

I can't stress this enough. Giving up something you love (your daydreaming) in favour of something you're not enjoying (your real life) is never going to work. The part of you that believes you deserve to be happy, the part of you that wants what's best for you, isn't going to allow it. And you don't want to silence that part of yourself. Because you deserve to reach your potential. You deserve to be happy and fulfilled and successful. And the only way that's going to happen is if you tune into the part of you that wants it – the part of you that currently wants to daydream.

If you don't like coming back to reality, the answer isn't to stop yourself leaving. The answer is to make reality somewhere you want to be.

YOU HAVE TO WORK ON REAL LIFE

When you work on getting your life in order, you change reality from a place you want to escape from into a place you want to be. And that might be all it takes to get your maladaptive daydreaming under control. In Chapter 10, we'll look at tips and tricks to control your daydreaming, but when you make real life somewhere you want to be, your maladaptive daydreaming might subside on its own. Developing a healthier relationship with your daydreaming might not be anywhere near as difficult as you expect, once your daydream world is no longer the only place you can be happy.

How do you get your life in order? You start by figuring out what you want. You can't go anywhere until you know where you're going, so you have to have some idea of what an exciting and compelling reality looks like for you. And your ideal reality is not going to be anything like the perfect daydream world you've created in your head.

REAL LIFE IS NOT PERFECT

As we've seen, daydreaming is often about making up for something that's lacking in real life. It's wish fulfilment. And so it's easy to think that if you could make your daydream a reality, you'd be happy. But would you? Our daydream lives tend to be perfect, and perfect is over-rated. I'm not saying that just because perfect is unrealistic; I'm saying it because you wouldn't want everything to be perfect all the time. Not really. Perfect doesn't push you out of your comfort zone. Perfect doesn't inspire you to grow or change or discover what you're capable of. Perfect would quickly become boring.

Of course, perfect is *also* unrealistic. So let go of the idea that you need the "perfect" life before you can be happy. It's not going to happen, and even if it did, it wouldn't make you happy for long.

However, you need to have a vision for your life that's compelling enough to inspire you to work toward it, because it's in doing the work that we find the greatest happiness. The sense of satisfaction you get from achieving a goal is directly proportional to the effort you had to put into it.

That's why having the perfect life in our daydreams can sometimes feel a bit hollow. We tell ourselves it's because it's not real, but, in fact, it's because we didn't have to work for it. Take a moment to think about the things you're most proud of in your real life. They're probably things you had to work for, right? Graduating from college, sticking to an exercise routine, saving up enough money to buy your own place. They're things that pushed you out of your comfort zone. Things that showed you that you're capable of more than you realized.

When we work hard to achieve something we didn't know we were capable of, we feel fulfilled in a way that simply isn't possible in a daydream. But we've got used to avoiding that sort of effort, because in our daydreams we can jump straight to the happy ending. We need to retrain our minds to see the joy in the journey, in making the effort, in showing up consistently and in doing the work to build the life we want.

HOW DO YOU WANT YOUR LIFE TO BE?

In Chapter 15, we'll look at how you can use your daydreaming to manifest a better life. But before you can do that, you have to know what makes you happy. If your maladaptive daydreaming has disconnected you from yourself for a long time, you might not know that. Don't worry. The worksheet that accompanies this chapter can help you.

Remember, your ideal real life probably won't look anything like your daydream life. But it does need to meet any unmet needs you identified in Chapter 8.

If you're still filling in the self-monitoring forms you began in Chapter 6, you'll have a good idea of how much time you spend daydreaming each day. And if you completed the worksheet that accompanies Chapter 6, you'll have thought about how much daydreaming might be healthy for you. That means you can estimate how much time you'll save once you're daydreaming at a healthy level. Now you need to decide what you're going to do with that time.

It's important that you have a plan to fill the time you're going to free up as you reduce your daydreaming. If you don't fill that time, then you're probably going to replace daydreaming with boredom. And boredom can be a powerful daydreaming trigger.

At least to begin with, you should plan to fill the time with things you *want* to do, rather than things you *should* do. When I tried to reduce my daydreaming so I could get more chores done around the house, I failed miserably. I don't like doing chores, so I resist doing them. And that resistance takes the form of – you guessed it – daydreaming. But when I started writing, it was much easier to reduce my daydreaming to make time. I was swapping one thing I enjoy for another thing that I enjoy just as much. Telling myself I can't daydream right now because I need to get some writing done is much easier and more successful than telling myself I can't daydream because I need to get some chores done.

By the end of this chapter, you'll have learned some specific strategies that will help you improve your life. And once you like being in reality, it will become easier to accept that your daydream world isn't real.

Address any coexisting problems

The first step in making real life worth coming back to is addressing any coexisting problems you have. As we saw in Chapter 5, maladaptive daydreaming rarely exists in isolation. Your doctor or therapist may not be familiar with maladaptive daydreaming, but they will be familiar with the common coexisting conditions. And most of those can be treated, or at least managed.

Even if you can't talk to your doctor about your maladaptive daydreaming, please ask them to help you manage your depression, ADHD, anxiety or whatever else you're struggling with. Being a maladaptive daydreamer adds another layer to your coexisting conditions, but it doesn't make you any less deserving of support, and it doesn't mean that established treatments, such as antidepressants and CBT, won't help you.

By addressing any coexisting conditions, you free up the mental resources you need to improve your life. And when you get your depression, anxiety or whatever else you're suffering from under control, real life can feel much more manageable.

If you've been a maladaptive daydreamer for a while, you might think all your difficulties are caused by your daydreaming. You might think your life would be OK if you weren't spending so much time lost in your imagination. But if you have both maladaptive daydreaming *and* depression, for example, then if you didn't daydream, you'd still be depressed and you still wouldn't be living the life you want to live.

But depression can be treated. As I explained in Chapter 6, I don't think antidepressants are a long-term solution. But they can be helpful in the short to medium term. They can take the edge off your depression while you improve your life. And when your life is better, your depression will be easier to manage.

If you're battling both maladaptive daydreaming and another condition, the first thing you should do is get help with the coexisting condition. You deserve to be mentally healthy. Admitting that you're struggling, and asking for help, is not weakness. It's an act of self-love.

Learn to tolerate discomfort

The second thing to work on is learning to tolerate discomfort. This is hard for maladaptive daydreamers. As we saw in Chapter 8, many of us never learned to sit with difficult emotions. We thought we didn't need to. We thought we could avoid uncomfortable feelings by escaping into a daydream.

But if daydreaming is the only way you manage difficult emotions, you're going to become dependent on it. It might be why your daydreaming became maladaptive. To overcome maladaptive daydreaming, you'll need to be able to experience emotional discomfort without resorting to daydreaming as an unhealthy coping mechanism.

Life is full of negative emotions. None of us avoid them completely. And we wouldn't want to. We feel negative emotions – anger, sadness, guilt, etc – for a reason. They're signals from our subconscious that something is wrong and needs to change. When we avoid our negative emotions by daydreaming, we temporarily escape the discomfort of the emotion, but we also ignore its message. And when we do that, our subconscious mind has to shout louder to get our attention. That's one reason why, when we use daydreaming as an escape, we tend to feel even worse when we snap back to reality. It isn't just the frustration we feel about the time we've wasted in the daydream, it's also the emotion we were trying to avoid forcibly letting us know it's still there.

Once we understand that our negative emotions serve an important purpose, we can stop fighting them. If we allow ourselves to feel them, we can listen to the message they're bringing. Then they will have served their purpose, and they'll go away. You don't get rid of negative emotions by suppressing them. You get rid of them by inviting them in and letting them pass through. When you feel a negative emotion, instead of trying to avoid it, get into the habit of asking it why it's showing up for you at this time.

As we saw in Chapter 8, emotions, by themselves, typically last about 90 seconds. If the emotion persists for longer than that, you're probably reinforcing it with the thoughts you're having about it. So how do you listen to the negative emotion and allow it to pass through without being overwhelmed by it?

MINDFULNESS TO MANAGE NEGATIVE EMOTIONS

Mindfulness is a skill that can help you in many different areas of life. We'll see later how you can use mindfulness to take control of your daydreaming, but in this section we're going to look at how mindfulness can help you tolerate negative emotions.

One of the lovely things about mindfulness is that anyone can learn to do it. There are free resources online that you can use to get started. I've included links to a few in the Resources section at the end of this book. There is no one right way to practise mindfulness, so don't be afraid to try different approaches until you find one that works for you.

Mindfulness can be a hard skill for daydreamers to master. If you're new to mindfulness, you might think it's about trying to quiet your mind – trying *not* to think – and that can be daunting for daydreamers because our minds are never still. But, in fact, there are many different kinds of mindfulness, and relatively few of them involve trying not to think.

When you first try mindfulness, it might be hard to shut off your daydreaming. That's normal. For non-daydreamers, sitting still with the eyes closed reduces external distractions and can help quiet the mind. But for daydreamers, removing external distractions just creates space for our big internal distraction – daydreaming. You might find that when you're trying to be mindful, your daydream continues to run in the background, knocking on the door of your attention every few minutes. Don't worry. Just accept that this is harder for you than it is for non-daydreamers, so it will take you a bit longer to get the hang of it.

A mindfulness technique that I've found helpful for tolerating negative emotions, is the three-minute breathing space.

THE THREE-MINUTE BREATHING SPACE

I first learned the three-minute breathing space as part of the mindfulness-based cognitive therapy (MBCT) course. This course teaches mindfulness in the context of managing mental-health problems. There's a similar, but more general, course called mindfulness-based stress reduction (MBSR). If you have the opportunity to take either course in person, I highly recommend it. Learning mindfulness techniques in a group setting can be helpful for daydreamers – most of us find it harder to daydream if we're in a room full of people. Additionally, the structured format of a formal course will hold you accountable and might even help you keep going if you find mindfulness hard in the beginning – as you almost certainly will.

If you can't find an MBCT or MBSR course near you, you can still learn the three-minute breathing space. There are many videos online that will walk you through it (I've included a link to one in the Resources section), or you can follow these instructions:

1. Make sure you're in a comfortable position, ideally sitting or lying down. If it feels OK, close your eyes. If closing your eyes makes you anxious, you can focus gently on a spot a short distance in front of you.
2. Begin by gently asking yourself how you're feeling in this moment. What thoughts are running through your mind? What emotions are you feeling? If you find it difficult to name the emotion, focus instead on how and where you feel it in your body. Is there a tightness in your chest? Heat in your face? A knot in your stomach? Don't judge how you're feeling or try to analyze or explain it. Just mentally describe it, without getting attached to any emotions that come up.
3. Once you have a sense of what's going on for you in this moment, turn your attention to your breath. Notice where you feel your breath most clearly. Is it the air moving in and out of your nose? Is it your chest rising and falling? Or do you feel your breath most clearly in your abdomen? It doesn't matter where you feel it, just bring your attention to that point. Don't try to control your breathing. Just notice it. Notice the sensation of the breath going in. And then notice the sensation of the breath going out. If other thoughts creep in, just mentally acknowledge them and then gently bring your attention back to your breath.
4. When you've been focussed on your breathing for about a minute, expand your attention to take in the rest of your

body. Remain aware of your breath, but also become aware of any other physical sensations – notice where your body is pressing down on whatever you're sitting or lying on, notice how your clothes feel against your skin, notice whether you're hot or cold, notice anywhere your muscles feel tight, etc. Fill your awareness with the experience of being present in this moment.
5. After a minute or two in this expanded state of awareness, slowly open your eyes. Remain still for a few seconds before gently getting up and carrying on with your day, trying to maintain the groundedness you experienced during the breathing space.

The whole process should take no more than three to five minutes, which means you can fit it into your day whenever you're feeling stressed or anxious. Ideally, while you're learning, you should aim to do at least three breathing spaces per day.

At first, you may spend more of your three-minute breathing space being distracted than being mindful. That's OK. You'll get better with practice. It's important not to judge yourself. Notice and celebrate your progress rather than dwelling on how hard it is or how distracted you were.

Mindfulness gives us a healthy way to manage negative emotions. Instead of escaping from them, we can acknowledge them in a curious, detached way that means they don't overwhelm us. We're able to hear the messages our emotions are bringing us, and therefore we can allow them to pass through and dissipate. Instead of being experiences we repress and fight against, they become thoughts and feelings that we can acknowledge and release.

It's natural to feel sad when something didn't work out the way you hoped. It's natural to feel angry when someone oversteps your boundaries. Mindfulness allows you to acknowledge those challenging emotions and meet them with compassion. That's a much healthier response than judging yourself for having those emotions, and trying to repress them.

Take a small step toward achievement

Now that you've begun to address any coexisting conditions you might be struggling with, and you've started to use mindfulness to help you manage difficult emotions, the next step in improving your life is to set yourself a goal.

Setting goals and working toward them is how you get intentional about improving your life. Your life doesn't magically improve just because you realize that it needs to. And although your circumstances will probably change if you sit around and wait for life to happen to you, there's no guarantee that change will be for the better. The best way to improve your life is to get clear about what you want and then do the work to make it happen. That can feel daunting if you've been avoiding life for a long time, but don't worry – we're going to break this down into small, easy steps.

WHY DO WE SET GOALS?

In our daydreams, we can instantly have anything we want. And that means we forget what it feels like to work toward something. The satisfaction we get from achieving a goal is proportional to the amount of effort it took to get there. When we skip straight to the end result, as we do in our daydreams, it can feel nice to have what we wanted, but it doesn't feel as deeply fulfilling as it would if we'd poured all our energy into achieving it. That's one of the reasons real life is more rewarding than a daydream.

When you set yourself a meaningful, challenging goal, and commit to it, it's likely to push you out of your comfort zone. And that's where real change happens. It's where you discover what you're truly capable of. Achievements that stretch you are the ones that make you proud. And when you're proud of yourself, it boosts your self-esteem and reduces shame. That process is impossible to replicate in a daydream.

The most compelling reason to set yourself a goal is that you need to give yourself something in real life that you can get excited about. We saw in Chapter 8 how maladaptive daydreaming is often a way to escape from something painful in your past. But fixing your past isn't enough. You need to get excited about the future.

Your mind wants to be active. Your mind wants to be motivated and to explore possibilities. If you don't satisfy that need in real life, you're going to look for it in your daydreams. By setting yourself a goal, you give yourself a challenge, something to strive toward, something to look forward to.

When you set yourself a goal that truly motivates and excites you, you discover that most of the joy is in the journey. Yes, the goal itself will be meaningful and inspiring, but you won't be putting in the work just because you want to achieve the end result; you'll be putting in the work because it's the work itself that adds meaning and depth and purpose to your life. Every step forward will make your life a little bit better. And every step forward builds momentum.

CHOOSE A GOAL

How do you decide what to work toward? If you haven't felt in control of the overall direction of your life for a long time, it can be hard to know where to start. You probably feel that there are a lot of things you'd like to change, and most of them feel overwhelming. The gap between where you are now and where you want to be might be so huge that it's discouraging rather than motivating, which might be one of the things that's driving your daydreaming.

That's why I want you to start small. Don't think about where you want to be a year from now or five years from now. Think about what you can realistically achieve in the next few weeks. You want to see progress quickly. The big audacious goals are absolutely within your reach, but they'll take time, and you need to generate some momentum by hitting some smaller goals first.

Your goal also needs to be something that is 100% under your control. It's important at this stage that you achieve your goals, because you want to give yourself the opportunity to notice how good it feels. That's what will give you the motivation to keep taking the action necessary to improve your life. Later on, you might set a goal that depends in part on other people, such as getting a promotion or winning a competition, but for now, stick to something where the outcome doesn't depend on anyone except you.

Finally, your goal needs to be something that stretches you enough to feel challenging but is easy enough that you know you can do it if you're willing to put in the effort. And it needs to excite you enough that you'll be willing to put in that effort. So it has to be something meaningful to you that you're going to enjoy working toward.

Don't worry if you're finding it difficult to come up with a goal that fits all of these criteria. The worksheet that accompanies this chapter will help you to generate some ideas.

COMMIT TO TAKING ACTION

Once you've chosen a goal, you need to commit to taking the action necessary to achieve it. A goal isn't a wish. Real life isn't a daydream. Things don't magically happen just because you imagine them.

So how do you motivate yourself to take action on your goal? The way to maintain motivation is to be able to see your progress. So break your goal down into tiny steps. Each step should be small enough that you can achieve it in one go. For example, if you've set yourself a goal of exercising twice a week, schedule both sessions in your diary. The satisfaction of ticking off the first one will motivate you to do the second one.

There are also a couple of ways you can use your daydreaming to motivate you. First, when you feel your motivation dipping, ask yourself whether your daydream self would quit so easily. My guess is that they wouldn't. As we'll see in Chapter 13, all the abilities that your awesome, capable daydream self has are already within you in some form. If your daydream self could achieve this small, manageable goal that you've set yourself, you certainly can.

Second, you can call on your daydream characters for motivation. Imagine having one of them sitting beside you while you're working on your goal. Do you want them to see you procrastinating, or do you want them to see you working to make your life better?

Once you've set your goal and taken action on it, stop and notice how it feels to have made that little bit of progress toward improving your life. It's noticing and celebrating your progress that will motivate you to keep going.

Build social connections

Humans are a social species. We are hard-wired to seek out meaningful connections with other people. We were born to collaborate, cooperate, exchange ideas and support each other. Put simply, we *need* other people in our lives.

Unfortunately, many maladaptive daydreamers have had relationships that were less than positive. The experiences that pushed our daydreaming into becoming maladaptive probably involved other people. Maybe someone hurt us, or someone wasn't there for us when we needed them. So we turned inward and discovered that we could form deep and meaningful connections with our characters.

Our relationships with our daydream characters can be profoundly nurturing and fulfilling. In Chapter 14, we'll look at how our daydream relationships can add meaning and depth to our real lives. But there are things our characters can't give us. No matter how beautiful our daydream relationships are, we *also* need real connections with real people.

WHY YOU NEED REAL-LIFE CONNECTIONS

There are several reasons why daydream relationships can never completely replace real-life relationships. One is that daydream relationships are all about you. Your daydream characters exist because *you* want them to. You don't have to consider their feelings. You don't have to compromise. You don't have to be OK with them having other friends. The relationship exists purely because of what *you* get out of it. That can feel good, it can bring a lot of love into your life, and it can even help you understand yourself better. But it doesn't broaden your perspectives, it doesn't bring an exchange of ideas, and it doesn't allow you to experience the joy of learning, working and growing together with another person.

As we've seen, daydreaming cannot push you out of your comfort zone. Your daydream friends don't challenge you. They don't help you to grow. They can be safe, dependable, loyal companions, but you also need people in your life who encourage you to become more than you already are. People who see the world from a different perspective and, in so doing, inspire you to consider new ideas and new ways of being. You aren't going to find those people in your daydreams.

If you've been maladaptively daydreaming for a long time, it's probably taken a toll on your social life. You might have turned down opportunities to socialize so you could spend more time daydreaming. You might have lost interest in activities and people you used to spend time with. You've probably let friendships drift away. Part of making real life worth coming back to is making real-life connections a priority again. You need to either recover past friendships or make new ones.

HOW TO REBUILD YOUR SOCIAL NETWORK

Making new friends can be daunting for maladaptive daydreamers. If your daydreaming became maladaptive in childhood, you probably didn't learn social skills at the same rate as your peers. You might feel anxious in social situations. You might feel you don't have much to talk about or that you're not an interesting person. Those concerns are common, even among non-daydreamers.

The thing is, the only way to improve your social skills is to practise. You have to force yourself to get out there and connect with people. That can be terrifying if you're not used to it, but there are ways to make it easier.

Resurrecting an old friendship that you've let slide is one possibility. If you were friends once, there's a good chance you can be again. After my breakdown, I reached out to several former friends who I hadn't spoken to in years. All of them were pleased to hear from me. Reconnecting with someone you've lost touch with is easier than you think. You could send an email, a text or even a letter. Tell them that you miss them and ask if they'd like to catch up sometime. You might find that they've been missing you too.

If you'd rather seek out new friends, try to find people who share your interests. Online groups are a good place to start. Or look for meetup groups in your local area. And don't discount work colleagues. You might not want to talk about work all the time, but your colleagues were drawn to the same career as you for a reason. Different professions attract different types of people. You and your colleagues might have more in common than just your job.

When you're trying to build your social network, accept any and all invitations to get out and socialize. Later on, when your social life is where you want it to be, you can be selective about what you agree to. But in the beginning, you need to take every opportunity to build those deeper connections you need. And don't always wait for the invitations to come to you. Be proactive. Text a friend and ask if they'd like to meet for coffee. Drop someone an email to let them know you're thinking about them. Comment on your friends' social media posts. Not everything you do will lead to a closer social connection, but over time you'll find that you'll develop deeper relationships with the people that matter most to you.

Having meaningful relationships leads to a sense of belonging and connectedness. And that can go a long way toward making real life a place you're happy to be.

Look after yourself

An important part of building a life you want to be present in is looking after yourself. As we saw in Chapter 7, most daydreamers struggle with shame, and one of the manifestations of shame is that it tells us we're not worth looking after, that our needs don't matter. When we think we're not worth it, self-care goes to the bottom of the priority list. And when we spend too much time daydreaming, we never get to the bottom of our priority list.

If you're reading this and realizing it's been a long time since you did anything nice for yourself, don't worry. You're not alone. Many daydreamers neglect even the most basic forms of self-care. It's hard to take pride in your appearance when you can't look at yourself in the mirror. It's hard to eat healthily when you don't plan your meals in advance. It's hard to get enough sleep when you can't stick to a consistent bedtime. Maladaptive daydreaming can interfere with all of those things.

While you're working on overcoming your maladaptive daydreaming, you need to find ways to look after yourself that don't involve daydreaming. Later on, when you've got your daydreaming under control, it might be possible to see daydreaming as a form of self-care. It might be part of how you unwind after a long day, for example. But while you're still having trouble controlling your daydreaming, particularly if you feel guilty or ashamed after daydreaming, then daydreaming isn't self-care. Something cannot be self-care if it's harming you – no matter how good it feels in the moment.

Self-care should reduce your stress levels and help you feel good about yourself. So don't put pressure on yourself to do too much. If you haven't prioritized self-care for a long time, start slowly. Pick one or two activities that might make a difference. Try them for a while and notice how you feel. You can always build more in later as you start to get your daydreaming under control.

Some of the simplest forms of self-care are the little things that send a signal to yourself that you matter. Your physical health and your mental health are connected, so when you look after your body, your mind will often be happier. Get dressed in clean clothes every day, shower regularly, brush your teeth, make healthier choices at the cafe or grocery store. These little things don't take much time, but they can make a surprisingly big difference to how you feel about yourself.

Try to do something purely for pleasure every day. You could have a long soak in a warm bath, put your feet up with a cup of tea and a magazine, get your nails done or watch something fun on TV – whatever helps you relax. The important thing is that you take time for *you*, and you don't feel guilty about it afterwards.

When you spend a lot of time daydreaming, it's easy to fall into the trap of believing you have to be productive in every non-daydreaming moment just to keep up with the things you need to do. But no one can be productive all the time. You need to be able to relax without daydreaming. Making time to do something just because you enjoy it might feel odd at first, but that's because you're not used to it. The more you practise, the more natural it will feel.

Making time for regular self-care will reduce your stress levels. And when your baseline level of stress is lower, you'll be better able to handle minor everyday stresses. Something that might once have been overwhelming enough to trigger a daydream might now feel more manageable.

When you make time for self-care, you send yourself a powerful message that you matter and that you deserve a better life. When you've been wading through shame for a long time, acknowledging that you matter is a huge step forward; make sure you celebrate it.

Worksheet: Set yourself a goal

The worksheet that accompanies this chapter will help you to identify one area of your life that you would like to work on over the next few weeks so that you can begin to make real life a place you want to come back to.

Download the worksheet at:
https://daydreamplace.com/extreme-imagination/worksheet-chapter9.pdf

CHAPTER 10

TAKING CONTROL OF YOUR DAYDREAMING

Before we dive into this chapter, I want you to take a moment to congratulate yourself. Hopefully by now you're beginning to understand what drives your maladaptive daydreaming, you've thought about how to make real life a place you want to come back to, and, most importantly, you're starting to release any shame you feel about being a maladaptive daydreamer.

Perhaps you've already noticed your daydreaming becoming easier to manage. But even if you haven't, I hope you're feeling happier, stronger and more empowered as a result of the work you've done so far. That's a significant step forward. I'm proud of you. And I hope you're proud of yourself – for committing to your recovery, for having the courage to do the hard work, and for having faith in your ability to overcome your maladaptive daydreaming.

Now that you have a solid foundation in place, you're ready to learn strategies to give you more control over your daydreaming. This chapter isn't intended to be a step-by-step guide. You don't have to do everything I suggest here. Some of these strategies won't work for you; others will be life-changing. Take the ideas that help you and combine them into a personalized plan to take your daydreaming from where it is now to where you want it to be.

Keep monitoring your progress

As you start to take control of your daydreaming, your self-monitoring forms become even more important. In Chapter 6, we looked at how self-monitoring helps you understand where you're starting from. As you work to overcome your maladaptive daydreaming, your self-monitoring forms will help you track your progress, so if you've stopped using them, it's time to restart. Even if you can't fill in a form every day, try to do at least two or three a week so that you have an idea of where you are.

As you overcome your maladaptive daydreaming, you'll have good days and bad days. That's normal. But the constant fluctuation can make it difficult to see trends. On a bad day, it will feel much harder to control your daydreaming than perhaps it did a week ago, and that can be de-motivating. You wonder if you're making any progress. But if you can look at your self-monitoring forms and see that *in total* you've daydreamed less this week than last week, despite the bad day, that can reassure you that your hard work is paying off. And that reassurance can motivate you to keep going.

If your definition of healthy immersive daydreaming includes a specific time goal – for example, that you'll daydream for no more than 30 minutes in the evening – your self-monitoring forms will be an essential tool in meeting that target. If there's a big gap between how much you're currently daydreaming and how much you want to daydream, you probably won't be able to hit your target immediately. But if you can see your daydreaming time falling week after week, you'll know you're on the right track.

As we saw in Chapter 6, overcoming maladaptive daydreaming will be easier if you have people supporting you. And hopefully, after using some of the strategies in Chapter 7, you're feeling more confident about talking to the people closest to you about your struggles. But if you're still doing this on your own, you're going to have to support and encourage yourself. Tracking your progress through self-monitoring is one way to do that. Alternatively, regularly journaling about your progress can help you see how well you're doing. Or if journaling doesn't appeal to you,

you could recruit one of your daydream characters to help. Schedule a check-in with them every week to talk specifically about your progress. As we'll see in Chapter 14, this type of "connected daydreaming" can help you move forward in many different areas of your life.

Managing your triggers

Completing your self-monitoring forms has probably increased your awareness of your triggers. You might already have known that certain things trigger your daydreaming – music, for example. But you might also have discovered some less obvious triggers. Let's look at some of the common daydreaming triggers and how you can manage them.

Before we start, let's get one thing clear: avoiding your triggers isn't healing, it's restricting. Trying to overcome maladaptive daydreaming by avoiding your triggers isn't addressing the problem, it's side-stepping it. Everything you've done up to this point has been about reducing your need to daydream. And one consequence of not *needing* to daydream is that you should be able to experience a trigger without reacting to it. Your goal is to break the connection between the trigger and the daydreaming, not to eliminate the trigger from your life.

In most cases, something has become a trigger because your mind has learned to associate it with daydreaming. If you've always daydreamed to music, for example, then your mind has learned that those two things go together. So when you hear music, your mind *expects* to daydream. Not daydreaming in that moment feels wrong. And so you daydream because, on some level, it feels like the right thing to do.

The solution is, therefore, to break the mental connection between the trigger and the daydreaming. You need to establish a new normal. For example, if music triggers your daydreaming, you need to train your brain to respond differently to music. You don't stop listening to music. And you don't stop daydreaming. But you do stop doing the two things together. For this reason, it's best to focus on one trigger at a time. If you normally put your headphones on, turn the music up loud and go for a walk while you daydream, then, as a first step, you still walk and daydream, but you don't listen to music while you do it. And when you listen to music, you make a determined effort not to daydream. Instead, you focus on being fully present with the music. The technique of present-moment awareness, which we'll cover later in this chapter, will help. If you find yourself daydreaming, immediately turn off the music.

This will feel hard at first. You're establishing a new habit. But as your mind lets go of the association between daydreaming and music, it will get easier. Eventually, you'll find you don't have to consciously focus on something while you listen to music. You'll be able to have it playing in the background while you do something else, without constantly feeling the urge to daydream.

EMOTIONAL TRIGGERS

If the trigger is an emotion, rather than something tangible, it can be a bit more difficult to manage. As we saw in Chapter 5, if your daydreaming is triggered by anxiety, for example, it can become so automatic that you don't even realize you're feeling anxious. The gap between feeling anxious and starting to daydream is so small that the anxiety doesn't have time to register in your conscious awareness. You just suddenly find yourself daydreaming. If that happens, as soon as you notice you're daydreaming, you need to stop and ask yourself why. Ask yourself what it is about reality in this moment that means you don't want to be there. Recording the answer on your self-monitoring form will help you spot repeating patterns.

When the trigger is an uncomfortable emotion, you need to find a healthier way to manage that emotion. As we saw in Chapter 9, mindfulness is one way to do that.

BOREDOM AND PROCRASTINATION

Other common daydreaming triggers are boredom and procrastination. If you've started to implement some of the strategies in Chapter 9 to make real life worth coming back to, boredom should be less of a problem than it used to be. But everyone experiences boredom occasionally. If your automatic response to boredom is to daydream, spend some time making a list of go-to activities that you can do instead. I find that listening to podcasts, playing the cello or doing a short mindfulness practice helps me resist the urge to daydream when I'm bored. I'm sure you can come up with your own list.

Procrastination is something we all struggle with. If you want to build a life you love, you'll eventually need strategies to avoid procrastination. But right now, your focus is on overcoming your maladaptive daydreaming. Fight one battle at a time. If you use daydreaming to procrastinate, the first step is to switch to another activity. Non-daydreamers have plenty of them: social media, video games, watching TV. I'm not suggesting any of those as a long-term strategy for daydreaming less, but the aim here is to break the connection between procrastination and daydreaming.

Finally, don't assume that there's always a trigger. For many of us, daydreaming is just our default state – it's what our minds do when we're not focussed on anything in particular. It may be hard to believe now, but once you have your daydreaming under control, that default daydreaming won't be a problem, because you'll be able to push it aside whenever real life needs your attention.

Resisting the urge to daydream

One of the big differences between immersive daydreaming and maladaptive daydreaming is that in immersive daydreaming, you're in control of your daydreams, whereas in maladaptive daydreaming your daydreams are in control of you. So one of the ways you'll know when you have overcome your maladaptive daydreaming is when you can choose when and for how long you daydream.

For daydreaming to become a choice, rather than something that overtakes you, you have to be able to resist the urge to daydream when you have something more important to do. That might feel impossible right now because when the urge to daydream strikes it probably feels overwhelming. But there are ways you can manage it and put yourself back in control.

First of all, let's be clear about what you *don't* do. When you feel an urge to daydream, you don't focus on fighting the urge. You don't say to yourself over and over *"Don't daydream. Don't give in to it."* All that does is focus your attention on how much you want to daydream. It's unlikely to work for more than a few seconds.

So what do you do instead? You start by getting curious about the urge. Why do you want to daydream right now? Did something trigger it? Are you bored? Are you avoiding something you don't want to do?

Once you understand what's pushing you toward daydreaming in this moment, you can make an informed decision as to whether you should give in to it. If there's nothing more productive you could be doing with this moment, you might decide it's OK to daydream for a while. That's your choice. *Choosing* to daydream puts you in control.

But if you decide that your best choice in this moment is *not* to daydream, your next step is to distract yourself by doing something that requires your full attention. Focussing your whole mind on something real when you desperately want to daydream will feel hard. But you don't have to do it for long. Two or three minutes will be enough to know whether distraction is going to work.

The best distraction, if there's someone else around, is to start a conversation with a real person. Talk to someone face-to-face if you can or, if that's not possible, pick up the phone and call someone.

If you're in a situation where talking to someone isn't possible, you could try the three-minute breathing space that you learned in Chapter 9. There's also a technique from DBT called 54321. You mentally name five things you can see, four things you can touch, three things you can hear, two things you can smell and one thing you can taste.

If you can remain focussed on something other than daydreaming for even a few minutes, you might find the urge to daydream passes and you can get on with your day. But if the urge persists, the next thing to try is becoming mindful of it. Allow yourself to experience the urge without giving in to it. Acknowledge that the urge is there. Notice what it feels like. Accept that you want to daydream *and* you're not going to daydream. You're not fighting the urge – that's important. You're not trying to get rid of it. You're allowing it to be there. And in so doing, you're learning that it's possible to feel the urge without giving in to it. This is called urge surfing. There's a link to more information about this in the Resources section.

If you successfully resisted the urge to daydream, don't forget to congratulate yourself. It's important to celebrate your successes. Even if you didn't manage to resist, congratulate yourself for trying. Every time you try to resist the urge, even if you don't succeed, you're making progress. Next time it will be easier.

Present-moment awareness

In Chapter 9, we looked at how mindfulness, and in particular the three-minute breathing space, can help you tolerate negative emotions instead of running away from them. But there are many other ways you can use mindfulness to help you overcome your maladaptive daydreaming.

Mindfulness has been scientifically shown to help reduce maladaptive daydreaming. The first scientifically validated treatment programme for maladaptive daydreaming used a combination of self-monitoring and mindfulness (Herscu et al., 2023). One-third of the study participants saw a significant improvement in their daydreaming; one-quarter improved so much that they no longer met the criteria for maladaptive daydreaming disorder.

Not all forms of mindfulness involve sitting still and paying attention to your breathing. There is something called present-moment awareness, which I have found to be helpful in managing my daydreaming. Present-moment awareness is the opposite of daydreaming. Whereas daydreaming disconnects you from reality, present-moment awareness holds you in reality. Present-moment awareness is easy to fit into your life, because it doesn't take any time. It's something you practise as you're going about your daily life.

One of my favourite ways to practise present-moment awareness is to walk in nature. I go to the local park, and, as I walk, I make a conscious effort to quiet my mind and just *notice*. I notice the leaves on the trees, the patterns the sunlight makes on the ground, stones in the path. I notice dogs barking, birds singing, children laughing. I notice how my body is moving – how it feels as each foot strikes the ground, how my weight subtly shifts from one side to the other as I walk, how the wind feels against my face. Once you start paying attention, there's a lot to notice. Don't start thinking about what you notice, just notice. Notice the sights, sounds and sensations, and then let them go. You don't quiet your mind, but you do shut off your thoughts.

Any activity can be an opportunity to practise present-moment awareness. You could try mindful eating by noticing everything about your food – how it looks on the plate, how it feels when you pick it up or push your fork into it, what it tastes like. Or you could wash dishes mindfully by paying attention to how the warm water feels against your skin, how the clean dishes sparkle as you stand them up to dry, what sensations you notice in your body as you stand at the sink, etc.

You can drop into present-moment awareness at any time throughout the day. It doesn't matter how long you do it for. To begin with, you'll probably be able to stay focussed for only a few seconds, but you can keep refocussing each time your mind wanders, until you feel more grounded.

Present-moment awareness gives you another way to manage your triggers. If you pace while daydreaming, mindful walking can help you break the mental association between pacing and daydreaming. Similarly, mindfully listening to music can help you break the connection between music and daydreaming.

As well as helping with your triggers, present-moment awareness can help you resist the urge to daydream. It can be used alongside the 54321 technique or as part of urge surfing. Present-moment awareness is a grounding technique that holds you in reality, or brings you back to reality if you've slipped into an unwanted daydream.

Allocating time to daydream

In Chapter 6 we discussed what overcoming maladaptive daydreaming might look like in the context of *your* life. For many daydreamers, that involves thinking about how much you want to daydream and when it might or might not be OK to daydream.

Remember, you're trying to reduce your daydreaming to a level where you can control it and make it work for you. You're not trying to eliminate it completely. Therefore, you need to find the level of daydreaming that's right for you.

I'm not going to tell you how much you should be daydreaming. That's up to you. Everyone's life is different. Finding a healthy level of daydreaming isn't about numbers. It's about tapping into the benefits of daydreaming without missing out on the benefits of being present in reality.

Even though it's not, ultimately, about numbers, tracking some numbers while you're recovering can be helpful. One way it helps is that it allows you to set aside a specific amount of time each day for daydreaming. One of the reasons that people who suddenly try to completely stop daydreaming almost never succeed is because when the urge to daydream strikes, there's nowhere for it to go. When you set aside specific times for daydreaming, it makes it easier not to daydream at other times. When you feel an urge to daydream, instead of telling yourself *"no"*, you tell yourself *"not yet"*.

AVOID DAYDREAMING OUTSIDE YOUR ALLOCATED TIME

Think about a typical day. When can you afford to spend some time daydreaming without it being a problem? How long can you daydream for while still doing everything else you need to do? Are there times in your day when there's nothing more productive you could be doing? Block out some specific times as "daydreaming time".

Try to give yourself some daydreaming time every day. Pushing the urge to daydream back until this evening is a lot easier than pushing it back until the weekend. You're more likely to succeed if you don't have to resist the urge too many times before you give in to it.

Be realistic! If you're currently daydreaming for six hours a day, you're not going to be able to cut it down to 15 minutes. Accept that in the beginning your brain will need a lot of daydreaming time, so give it as much as you can. You can cut down further as you progress with your recovery.

Once you've decided when and where it's OK to daydream, you need to focus on avoiding daydreaming at other times. How will you manage a daydreaming urge outside of your allocated daydreaming time? Telling yourself there's time to daydream later will often work, but if the urge doesn't go away, you'll need to use the strategies we explored earlier in this chapter.

Something that I've personally found helpful, but which works only because I have allocated daydreaming time, is asking one of my daydream characters to hold me accountable. If I start daydreaming outside my allocated time, I imagine my character saying "*No. We agreed we're not doing that now. We can come back to it later.*" It's hard to continue daydreaming when your characters are refusing to cooperate.

STOP DAYDREAMING WHEN YOUR TIME IS UP

To successfully restrict your daydreaming to your allocated time, you have to be able to stop daydreaming when the time is up. If you've decided to stop daydreaming at a specific time, you need to set an alarm. Time passes differently in the daydream world, and your time will be up before you realize.

But how do you stop daydreaming when the alarm goes off? First, stop any physical activities that are associated with your daydreaming. If you pace, sit down. If you listen to music, turn it off. If you fidget with a special object, put it away.

Second, practise closing out the daydream the same way every single time. Have one sentence that always ends your daydream. Perhaps you tell your characters "*That's it until next time*", or "*I need to go now, I'll be back later*", or "*Let's leave that as a cliffhanger for the next episode.*" Pick whatever works for you and use it at the end of every daydream from now on. That will send a signal to your brain that daydreaming time is over.

Finally, if it's still hard to leave the daydream, use the 54321 technique we looked at earlier in this chapter to bring you firmly back to reality. Follow it up immediately with some of the other techniques you use to resist a daydreaming urge.

If your allocated daydreaming time is brought to an end by something outside your control – for example, when the bus gets to your stop – you might have an additional problem. You might be right in the middle of a compelling scene. The urge to return to a daydream that's been interrupted at a key moment can be huge. But do not be tempted to "just finish this scene" – trust me, that almost never works. You will go way over your allocated time before you realize it. Use the urge-reduction techniques we covered earlier in this chapter to manage the urge to continue daydreaming. It will feel *really* difficult at first, but knowing that you can come back to that scene later will help.

HOW TO COPE WITH A RELAPSE

As you start to put limits around your daydreaming, there will be times when you don't stick to them. Sometimes you'll decide to daydream for an hour, and one hour will become three. Or you'll decide not to daydream until after work, only to find yourself pacing around the block in your lunch break. When this happens, the important thing is to be gentle with yourself. You're establishing a new habit. Slip-ups are inevitable. It's what you do afterwards that matters. You need to make sure that the relapse doesn't derail your whole recovery. So how do you do that?

First, you need to forgive yourself. Relapses will happen. You aren't going to overcome maladaptive daydreaming overnight, and recovery is not a linear process. Some days it will all go wrong. That's OK. It doesn't mean you can't be successful in the long term.

Second, you should reflect on why you couldn't stick to your allocated time today. Were you feeling overly emotional? Did something upsetting happen that you needed to daydream to escape from? Were you bored? Think about whether the circumstances that led to your relapse are likely to happen again. If they are, you need to consider how you can respond in a healthier way next time. But if something out of the ordinary happened and caught you off guard, then the relapse was probably inevitable and you just need to accept it and move on.

Third, review how much progress you've made in overcoming your maladaptive daydreaming. Remind yourself why you're committed to taking back control of your mind. Put this one bad day in context by thinking about all the positives in your recovery journey.

Fourth, put the relapse behind you and recommit to the process.

If you record all of this on your self-monitoring form, then the next time you slip up you can remind yourself that this has happened before and you kept going.

GRADUALLY REDUCING YOUR ALLOCATION

As you get better at limiting your daydreaming to your allocated time, you'll be able to judge whether the amount of time you've allocated is right for you. If the urge to daydream outside your allocated time isn't diminishing at all, you might need more daydreaming time, at least for the moment. But if you still aren't meeting all of your responsibilities in real life, you might need to cut your daydreaming back further. Don't be afraid to keep adjusting it until you find a level that feels manageable and healthy.

If there's a big gap between the amount of time you're currently daydreaming and your estimate of what's healthy for you, you won't be able to cut down all in one go. You'll need to reduce it in stages. I'd recommend spreading the process over at least three months. It's a good idea to set small weekly targets. For example, if you're currently daydreaming for 4 hours a day and you'd like to reduce it to an hour, your target for next week might be 3 hours 45 minutes, and then 3 hours 30 minutes the week after and so on. Reducing your daydreaming by 15 minutes per day each week might not sound like much (and hopefully it won't feel like much), but by the end of three months, you'll be down to one hour a day. Setting yourself manageable short-term targets stops the process feeling overwhelming, while allowing you to see your progress and stay motivated.

Give yourself rules to follow

One of the ways you can nudge your daydreaming habits in the right direction is by making rules for yourself. Creating your own rules is a personal process. I'm not going to tell you when you should or shouldn't daydream. The definition of healthy immersive daydreaming is different for everyone, so I can't decide what is or isn't OK for you. And if you set your own rules, you're more likely to stick to them. When you make your own rules, you understand *why* those rules are important, and if you break them, the only person you're cheating is yourself.

Your daydreaming rules should be things you can realistically do that will help you avoid daydreaming when you don't want to. Think about the times and situations when you're tempted to daydream, and *why* it's so tempting to daydream at those times. Then think about what you'd like to do instead.

One of my rules is that I don't daydream when I'm in the same room as another person. I came up with this rule because I wanted to avoid zoning out during conversations. I wanted to improve my real-life relationships by giving the people around me the gift of my undivided attention. Every time I felt an urge to daydream while I was with somebody, I would remind myself that my daydream characters are always available but this real person is choosing to spend this moment of their life with me. So right now, they need to take priority.

As I practised not daydreaming around other people, I noticed another benefit of this rule. I was training my mind to believe I had to be alone in order to daydream. And that gave me another way to resist a daydreaming urge. If I was being pulled into a daydream, I could distract myself by finding a real person to have a conversation with. What started out as a way to deepen my real-life relationships became a tool I could use to resist an urge to daydream.

This illustrates how making rules for yourself helps to retrain some of your automatic responses. Your rules become the foundation on which you establish habits, and you can use those new habits to help you respond differently to some of your daydream triggers.

Start your day grounded in reality

Most daydreamers wake up every morning and immediately want to daydream. My daydream characters are the first thing I think of when I wake up, and the urge to check in with them is huge. Wanting to daydream as soon as you wake up is so common that it features on the MDS-16.

If you start daydreaming the minute you wake up, it can easily derail your entire day. Daydreaming while you're still in bed makes it ten times harder to get up, so you'll stay in bed much later than you intended. And if you're distracted by your daydream while you're getting ready for your day, everything – showering, getting dressed, eating breakfast – will take twice as long. You'll be running late, which will generate a whole load of unnecessary stress. And given that stress is a powerful daydreaming trigger for most of us, you can see where that's going to lead. Giving in to the urge to daydream first thing in the morning will likely leave you fighting the urge the entire day.

If you've been struggling with maladaptive daydreaming for a while, that picture will be all too familiar. You've probably already realized how much easier life would be if you could get up and out in the morning without daydreaming.

So how do you do that? The most important thing you need to do is get out of bed the minute the alarm goes off. While you're lying in bed, you have only two options: go back to sleep or start daydreaming. You need to avoid both.

DEVISING A MORNING ROUTINE

Once out of bed, you need to go straight into a carefully crafted morning routine, which allows you to get up without being distracted by your daydreaming. What your ideal morning routine consists of will be personal to you, but here are a few things to consider.

First, you need to build in something mentally challenging enough to hold your attention so you don't start daydreaming, but not so challenging that it feels impossible while you're still half asleep.

Second, exercise can be a great way to start your morning. When you wake up, your levels of cortisol – one of the stress hormones – are at their highest. This is why some people feel anxious in the morning.

Stress and anxiety can be daydreaming triggers. Exercise helps your body use up that extra cortisol and can therefore make you feel calmer.

Third, mindfulness can ground you in reality and make your daydream world feel a bit more distant. If meditation is too difficult first thing in the morning, you could try present-moment awareness or journaling.

Fourth, if you can, get outside. Bright natural daylight signals to your body that it's time to start the day. It can help you feel alert more quickly, so you'll be better able to use the strategies you've learned in this chapter to manage any lingering urge to daydream.

Finally, the most important thing about your morning routine is you have to enjoy it. The first decision you'll make every day is whether to get up and do your morning routine or stay in bed and daydream. Your morning routine has to be enticing enough to win that battle.

The way I combine all of the above elements is by going outside and doing 15 minutes of tai chi as soon as I wake up. If that sounds like something you want to try, I've included a link to the routine I use in the Resources section. But if tai chi isn't your thing, that's OK. If you have the energy, you could go for a run. If not, you could make yourself a cup of coffee and sit quietly for a few minutes, journaling or planning your day. Experiment and find what works for you.

Your morning routine doesn't have to take long. Mine takes 15 minutes. But even if you can spare only five to ten minutes, it's probably enough. And if you think how many times you're currently hitting the snooze button, you'll probably realize that you can make time for a quick morning routine without setting the alarm any earlier.

I recommend not checking your phone until after you've done your morning routine. If that feels impossible, then at least make sure you get out of bed before you pick up your phone. You need to get your day started before you invite any stress into it.

Ultimately, it doesn't matter how you start your day, as long as you find something that will reliably get you out of bed without daydreaming. Like all the other habits you're developing as you overcome your maladaptive daydreaming, this will feel hard at first. But stick with it. As you establish your morning routine, you'll see just how much better the rest of the day flows when you can get up without daydreaming. That, in itself, will be a powerful motivation to continue with your morning routine.

Daydream relationships

Throughout this book, I've emphasized that what you daydream about is a lot less important than the effect your daydreaming has on you. But there's one thing almost all of us daydream about that deserves a mention because it can spill over into how you show up in real life, and that's daydream relationships.

It's almost inevitable that at some point you will daydream about being romantically involved with someone you're not dating in real life – whether that's someone you have a crush on, a celebrity you admire, a fictional character or even someone you made up. Because it's so common, in this section we're going to focus on romantic daydream relationships, but most of this advice is equally applicable to any daydream relationship; for example, a daydream parent or mentor, a daydream best friend, a daydream sibling or any other person you have a close connection with in your daydreams.

Daydream relationships are addictive because although the relationship isn't real and the other person may not be real, the emotions involved are very real. It *is* possible to fall in love with someone who exists only in your imagination. And love is love, regardless of whether the recipient is real or not. Your brain doesn't distinguish between fantasy and reality. All those feel-good chemicals that your body releases when you fall in love with a real person are also released when you fall in love with a figment of your imagination. And for that reason, a daydream relationship can be a beautiful thing.

REAL-LIFE RELATIONSHIPS VERSUS DAYDREAM RELATIONSHIPS

Although the emotions may be the same, real-life relationships and daydream relationships are completely different. They serve different purposes. And that means they don't necessarily compete with each other. It's possible to be dating someone in real life while having a daydream relationship with someone else. Sometimes that will be problematic; for example, if you neglect your real-life partner in favour of your daydream partner. But it isn't automatically something to avoid. If you can comfortably juggle a real-life relationship and a daydream relationship, you don't need to feel guilty about it. I personally don't think being in a daydream relationship automatically means you're cheating on your real-life partner. But for some people it can feel that way. If it feels like cheating to you, then perhaps that's a sign you shouldn't be doing it. But it's a personal decision.

However, if you feel you can't have a real-life relationship because you'd be cheating on your daydream partner, that's a problem. Real-life relationships are important. If your daydream relationship is causing you to withdraw from reality and reduce your social contacts, then it's not helping you. Real life has to come first.

I wouldn't recommend trying to have a real-life relationship and a daydream relationship with the same person. As we saw in Chapter 1, you can't put a real person in your daydreams. As soon as you try, they become a character, albeit a character based on someone real. They're not the real person you based them on; they're the person you want them to be, or perhaps the person the plot requires them to be. But if you're in a relationship with the person you based that character on, it's easy to blur the boundaries. You'll start expecting the real person to behave like the version of them you've created in your head. And that's eventually going to cause problems.

ARE DAYDREAM RELATIONSHIPS HEALTHY?

Daydream relationships can be beautiful. They can add meaning and depth to your life. They're safe. You have total control, which means you have the security of knowing the relationship will last as long as you need it to. Your daydream partner can love you unconditionally, they can be there for you whenever you need them, they can argue with your inner critic, and they can gently and lovingly support you in everything you do.

There are also downsides to daydream relationships. Daydream relationships are all about you. You never have to compromise. You never have to consider your partner's needs. You never have to see their point of view. Daydream relationships, wonderful though they are, don't prepare you for real-life relationships and can never fully replace them. You still need real-world connections, no matter how beautiful your relationship is with your daydream partner.

There are situations in which a daydream relationship can cause significant problems and you should consider ending it. You shouldn't tolerate anything in a daydream relationship that you wouldn't tolerate in a real-life relationship. It can sometimes be helpful to use your daydream world as a safe space to work through real-life trauma. But if that real-life trauma is the foundation of your daydream relationship, then the relationship may not be helping you work through it so much as keeping you stuck in it.

It's also unhealthy to expect your real-life relationships to be as perfect as your daydream ones. Real-life relationships aren't meant to be perfect. The magic comes from growing together with another person, and that process involves a fair amount of argument, compromise and working to understand each other – none of which is necessary with your "perfect" daydream partner. It's OK to have perfect in a daydream, but it's unrealistic to expect it in real life.

LIMERENCE

If your daydream partner is based on someone you'd like to be in a relationship with in real life, you need to be careful that it's a daydream relationship and not limerence. Limerence and daydream relationships are different, but being a daydreamer can make limerence worse. In a healthy daydream relationship, you can mentally separate your daydream partner from the person you based them on. You can let the real person get on with living their life, because your daydream relationship is enough for you. But with limerence, your daydreams are a mental rehearsal for something you hope will happen in real life. You obsessively gather as much information as you can about the real person, and you feed all of that into your daydreams. When you're experiencing limerence, you give your power away to someone real, someone you can't control. How you feel depends on how they behave. And that can lead to heartbreak.

To overcome limerence, you have to clearly separate the real person from the version in your head. Remember that you're mentally dating a daydream character. They're not the person you based them on. Let the real person get on with their life – stop following them on social media, stop thinking about where they'll be and what they'll be doing at any given moment. What you then do with the version in your head is up to you. You might be able to continue a daydream relationship with the character inspired by your limerence or you might not. You have to decide what's right for you.

ENDING A DAYDREAM RELATIONSHIP

If you decide that your daydream relationship isn't healthy, it's up to you to end it. Your daydream partner isn't going to break up with you. But how do you go about ending a relationship with someone who doesn't exist?

You can't just stop daydreaming about someone, particularly if they've been in your daydreams for a while. You have to deliberately end it. If you try to just forget about them, it will feel as though you have unfinished business, and that will keep pulling you back. You have to break up with your daydream partner in the same way you would if it was someone real. You need to daydream a break-up scene with them. Explain exactly why you've decided the relationship has to end. Your break-up scene will probably make you cry. That's OK. It's natural to grieve the ending of something that was a big part of your life and meant a great deal to you.

Once you've done your break-up scene, you have to be strict with yourself about going back. If that person pops up in your daydreams again, remind them (and yourself) that you broke up. Don't be tempted to revisit earlier scenes where you were still together. You might even have to create a completely new plot if your daydream partner was too entrenched in the old one.

In the days and weeks after the break-up scene, be kind to yourself. It will feel similar to ending a real relationship, but you probably won't have as much support as you would after a real break-up. So you have to provide your own support. Focus on self-care. And don't judge yourself for needing time to get over it. The relationship wasn't real but your feelings were. It's OK to be sad when something beautiful ends.

Daydream relationships don't challenge you or inspire you to grow in the way real-life relationships do. For that reason, they can never fully take the place of real-life relationships. But that doesn't mean that daydream relationships can't be wonderful things in their own right. You *can* be in love with a character you created. And that love can be real. Don't judge yourself for having feelings – it's your feelings that make you human.

> ### Worksheet: Your personalized action plan
>
> The worksheet that accompanies this chapter will help you to identify which of the strategies we've discussed will be most helpful to you. You'll then develop your own personalized action plan to take control of your maladaptive daydreaming.
>
> Download the worksheet at:
> https://daydreamplace.com/extreme-imagination/worksheet-chapter10.pdf

CHAPTER 11

BRINGING IT ALL TOGETHER

We've covered a lot of material in the last five chapters, so in this chapter we're going to review the four components of sustainably healing from maladaptive daydreaming. I'll also describe how these strategies helped me to overcome my own maladaptive daydreaming.

The four steps to overcoming maladaptive daydreaming

As we've seen, there are four key aspects to overcoming maladaptive daydreaming, which we covered in Chapters 7–10.

DROP THE SHAME

First, you need to understand how shame contributed to your daydreaming becoming maladaptive, and you need to release the shame you feel about being a daydreamer. We've looked at why holding on to shame will interfere with your healing process by putting up a barrier between you and the world you're trying to come back to. As long as you feel shame about your daydreaming, you'll always want to hide it, and it will become the secret that stops you from living fully and authentically in reality. We discussed why being ashamed of your daydreaming creates an inner conflict because you try to repress part of who you are. And we learned that the antidote to shame, difficult though it is, is to stop hiding the thing you're ashamed of.

If you haven't already told at least one person, in real life or online, about your struggles with maladaptive daydreaming, I want you to address that right now. Use some of the goal-setting techniques we learned in Chapter 9 to make a plan to tell someone about your daydreaming. And then commit to following through on that plan. It's hard, but it's important. If you don't start to release the shame you feel about your daydreaming, you're making the rest of the process so much harder. Opening up to other people is the best way to release shame.

UNDERSTAND WHAT YOUR DAYDREAMING IS DOING FOR YOU

Once you begin to release the shame, you then need to look at what your daydreaming is doing for you. Your maladaptive daydreaming persists because it's either allowing you to escape from something you can't cope with any other way or meeting a need that isn't being met anywhere else. While that situation persists, your daydreaming is serving a purpose and you won't be able to give it up.

If you're escaping from a problem or situation, what steps have you taken to either resolve it or at least cope with it in a healthier way? If your daydreaming has been meeting a need, what are you doing to get that need met in real life? If you don't have good answers to those questions, your daydreaming is still in control. You still need it more than you need to be free of it.

MAKE REAL LIFE WORTH COMING BACK TO

As you reduce your reliance on your daydreaming, you need to make real life a place you want to come back to. In Chapter 9, we looked at how you can address some of the challenges that come with being a maladaptive daydreamer: poor mental health, a lack of healthy coping skills, feeling as though you're falling behind in life, being socially isolated and not taking care of yourself. We looked at some self-coaching techniques that can help you to overcome these problems and build a fulfilling and satisfying life.

TAKE CONTROL OF YOUR DAYDREAMING

Finally, in Chapter 10, we looked at some tips and tricks that will give you more control over your daydreaming. We revisited the importance of self-monitoring, learned how present-moment awareness can ground you in reality and discussed how to manage your triggers. We also looked at the common problems of daydreaming first thing in the morning and being in an unhealthy daydream relationship.

HOW TO BRING THE STEPS TOGETHER

Everyone experiences maladaptive daydreaming differently. And so everyone's solution will be different. The four components are the foundation on which you can build your own personalized recovery programme.

Although it's important that you read and understand each of the four steps before moving on to the next one, it isn't essential to complete them in order. You can, and probably should, work on all four steps together. Some of the changes you'll make as you work through this process will become lifelong habits. Being an immersive daydreamer is a gift, but it comes at a price. You will *always* have to guard against your daydreaming becoming maladaptive again. That risk never goes away. And that means you'll need to be aware of your mental health and proactive about managing it.

Ultimately, the only person who can overcome your maladaptive daydreaming is you. As we've seen, you can and should ask for support, but you're the one in charge. You have to take responsibility. I've shown you the way, but you have to walk the path. It won't be easy or quick. But if you commit to the process, the rewards will go far beyond taking control of your daydreaming. When you release your shame, heal your trauma and work on real life, *every* aspect of your life will improve.

How this process changed my life

I first developed maladaptive daydreaming in childhood, as a way to cope with loneliness and social isolation. I lost most of my teenage years to maladaptive daydreaming. And as an adult, my daydreaming oscillated between immersive and maladaptive for decades. When real life was going well, I didn't need to daydream as an escape, so I was free to enjoy it. But when life became challenging, I ran away from those challenges by daydreaming, and it became maladaptive.

It never occurred to me that I could control my daydreaming. I just accepted that it came and went on its own timescale – a bit like my depression. I never thought of it as something I had a choice about.

It wasn't until I was in my mid-40s that I learned that maladaptive daydreaming had a name and that other people do it too. That discovery helped me to see my maladaptive daydreaming for what it is – a mental disorder that can be treated and managed. I learned that I'm susceptible to maladaptive daydreaming because I'm an immersive daydreamer, but that immersive daydreaming itself isn't a problem. In fact, as we'll see in the next part of this book, it can be a beautiful gift.

I was fortunate. By the time I learned about maladaptive daydreaming, I'd had a lot of therapy for depression. I understood mental illness. And I'm insatiably curious about how the human mind works. When I realized I wasn't the only person in the world to have stories bouncing around in my head all the time, I wanted to learn more. I wanted to understand why my brain does this and how I could use it to my advantage.

By that point in life, I wasn't looking for a quick fix. I was married with children, and I'd done OK in my career. Maybe I could have achieved more if I hadn't been a maladaptive daydreamer, but overall I was content with where I was. So I never felt I needed to get rid of my daydreaming completely. I never went to war with myself.

I wasn't daunted when I realized that maladaptive daydreaming is usually a symptom of a deeper problem. I'd had enough therapy for my depression to know that I was dealing with some complex issues. It made sense that with everything I was managing, I needed to mentally check out sometimes. So the realization that overcoming maladaptive daydreaming meant sorting out my life and healing from my past trauma was more exciting than terrifying.

And the shame? I used to have a lot of shame about being a daydreamer. For most of my life, I couldn't tell *anyone*, because I thought they'd reject me as some kind of weirdo. As my mother used to say, "talking to yourself is the first sign of madness". And I wasn't just talking to myself. I had a whole crowd of characters that I talked to. Except that, as a child, I daydreamed in third person, so the people I was talking to didn't even know I existed. It never occurred to me that anyone else could daydream the way I did. I was different. And I grew up thinking that different was bad.

The day I learned about maladaptive daydreaming, the shame started to fall away. I wasn't alone. Other people had stories in their heads too. And that meant it wasn't just about me. It wasn't a sign of my unique inadequacy as a human being. I just had a brain that was wired a bit differently from the average.

Everything I've walked you through in this part – dropping the shame, understanding what you're escaping from, making real life worth coming back to and taking control of your daydreaming – has been a fundamental part of my own daydreaming journey. It's been six years since I started trying to understand and manage my daydreaming, and I'm still learning new things about how my mind operates. But my daydreaming is almost completely immersive now. I have days when it gets the better of me and I zone out more than I want to, but I have strategies to manage it. It's been a slow process. But the transformation has been huge. My life and my mental wellbeing are better now than I could ever have imagined. And my daydreaming has become my greatest gift.

You have a beautiful life to look forward to

You aren't going to overcome your maladaptive daydreaming today, or this week, or even this month. It will take time, and effort, and commitment. It won't be easy, because nothing worth having ever is. But trust me when I say that being an immersive daydreamer is one of the most beautiful and magical things about you. It's a gift. It allows you to see the world in a way that most people can't. And when you get your maladaptive daydreaming under control, you'll be free to appreciate that gift. That's what the final part of this book is all about – learning to love your awesome imagination.

SELF-MONITORING WON'T LAST FOREVER

You might be finding that the most tedious part of your recovery is filling in your daily self-monitoring forms. Hopefully you understand why these are so important, but you'll also be relieved to hear that you don't have to do them forever. So when can you stop?

Ultimately, like everything else in your recovery process, it's up to you. I recommend you continue until you've been *consistently* implementing your recovery plan for at least a month. This is long enough to assess whether your plan includes all the elements you need to work on and to see a noticeable reduction in your daydreaming. A month is also long enough for some of your actions to become habits. If everything is going well, you can experiment with stopping self-monitoring. You can always start again if your recovery falls off track.

After you stop completing daily self-monitoring forms, you should schedule a time at least once a month to review your progress. Put it in your diary if you have to. Treat it as what it is – an important appointment with yourself. Spend some time honestly assessing where you're at, both with your daydreaming and with your life more generally. Are you making progress on your goals? If not, do you need to adjust your strategy? Are your goals still in alignment with the person you want to become and the life you want to live? Are they still motivating you? Do you need to set new goals? Taking time every month to reflect and reset is something that I've found to be the key to consistently moving forward.

BELIEVE IN YOURSELF

Before we move on to Part 3 and exploring the benefits of immersive daydreaming, I want to take a moment to say well done. If you've followed the strategies in this section, even if only for a short time, you should have a bit more control over your daydreaming. You should be feeling more optimistic about building a life you love. You should be able to imagine a future where you're free of maladaptive daydreaming, and that future should feel realistic and achievable. Compare that with how you were feeling when you first picked up this book. You've come a long way.

Overcoming maladaptive daydreaming is a massive achievement. It might be the hardest thing you've ever undertaken. But with enough determination and persistence, you can do it. I believe in you. I believe you're worthy of a life free from maladaptive daydreaming, and I hope that you can believe that too.

There's no limit to what you can achieve. Everyone has what it takes to build a life they love. All you need to do is get clear about what you want and consistently take the action necessary to achieve it. In Part 3, we'll look at how you can use your gift of immersive daydreaming to help you do exactly that.

Worksheet: Reflect on your progress

The worksheet that accompanies this chapter is an invitation to review what you've learned so far and assess the progress you've made in overcoming your maladaptive daydreaming.

Download the worksheet at:
https://daydreamplace.com/extreme-imagination/worksheet-chapter11.pdf

PART 3

LEARNING TO LOVE YOUR IMAGINATION

CHAPTER 12

LEARNING TO LOVE YOUR DAYDREAMING

In overcoming maladaptive daydreaming, you've let go of any shame you felt about your daydreaming, you've learned what was driving your maladaptive daydreaming, and you've started to improve your life. You've also learned some tips and tricks to give you more control over your daydreaming. Hopefully, you're now at the point where your daydreaming no longer rules your life. In this third and final part of the book, we're going to explore the benefits you can get from your daydreaming now that it's no longer maladaptive. We're going to look at how being an immersive daydreamer can enhance your life in ways you never imagined.

What we'll cover in this part of the book

In the next four chapters, you'll learn how you can use your daydreaming to increase your self-esteem, reconnect with your authentic self and move your life in the direction you want to go.

In Chapter 13, we'll look at how your daydream self can be a refuge for your authentic self, which is something many of us lost touch with a long time ago. Authenticity is incredibly important. I believe it's not possible to be truly happy if you're constantly pretending to be someone you're not. And your daydreaming is part of that. Our society sends us the message that daydreaming is unhelpful and unproductive and something you need to repress. Too many of us hear that message, and we try to repress a part of who we are. That's not healthy. Equally, however, you are so much *more* than just a daydreamer, and if you've been disconnected from reality and from your true self for a long time, it can be hard to figure out who you really are. Your daydream self can help you with that.

In Chapter 14, you'll learn how to bring some of your most important daydream characters out of the plot. By taking your characters out of the daydream world and into your reality, you can create a team of mental supporters who will motivate and encourage you in every aspect of your daily life.

In Chapter 15, we'll look at how you can use your daydreaming to enhance your day-to-day life. You'll learn to use your daydreaming to manage your emotions and thereby become more confident and emotionally resilient than you ever imagined possible. We'll look at the differences between daydreaming and manifesting, and why daydreamers can be master manifestors. You'll learn how to set up a mental safe space and why you need one, and you'll learn how to use your daydreaming to navigate the ups and downs of real-life relationships.

Finally, in Chapter 16, we'll look at how you can avoid slipping back into maladaptive daydreaming, as well as what you have to look forward to now that you've reclaimed control of your mind.

Your daydreaming is different now

Let's revisit the differences between immersive daydreaming and maladaptive daydreaming. The worksheet that accompanies Chapter 3 lists some of the key differences, but as your daydreaming gradually changes from maladaptive to immersive, there are some specific things you're likely to notice.

First, you'll be more accepting of your daydreaming as just part of who you are. When your daydreaming was maladaptive, you might have seen it as something you needed to eliminate from your life. As you transition back to immersive daydreaming, you realize that your daydreaming was never the problem, the problem was the effect your daydreaming was having on the rest of your life. As you get your daydreaming under control, and as you start to improve your life, you realize that you can overcome maladaptive daydreaming without having to fundamentally change who you are or how you think. You realize that it's OK to be a daydreamer.

Second, you'll stop feeling guilty about daydreaming. When you were daydreaming too much, it was natural, even healthy, to feel guilty about daydreaming when you should have been doing something else. That guilt was one of the signals that your daydreaming was out of control. But as you gain more control over your daydreaming, you daydream only when you genuinely have time for it, so there's no need to feel guilty.

Third, your daydream life and your real life will come into balance. Your daydreaming is no longer something you use to escape from reality. As an immersive daydreamer, you know that you have almost as much control over your real life as you do over your daydream life. In real life, you don't get everything you want instantly, but you can enjoy the challenge of working toward it, and you can become a better person along the way. You don't need to avoid real life by escaping into a daydream, because real life can be an exciting and fulfilling place to be. And that means it's OK that your daydream world isn't real.

Fourth, you'll be able to daydream because you *want* to rather than because you *need* to. And that means you'll be in control of your daydreaming rather than it being in control of you. Your need to be in control was one of the compelling things about your daydream world, so feeling more in control in reality – being able to choose when to daydream and when not to – is a precious thing.

Finally, as you overcome all the negative aspects of your daydreaming, you'll start to see immersive daydreaming as the gift that it is. You'll be free to enjoy all of the positives without suffering from the negatives. You'll start to appreciate what a powerful tool your imagination is. And that's what this part of the book is all about – learning to love your wild, beautiful, awe-inspiring imagination.

Immersive daydreaming is a form of play

Immersive daydreaming is an outlet for your natural creativity. Unlike the activities we share with the world, such as writing, art, music or whatever you do to express your creativity, daydreaming is an internal process, which means no one else gets to judge whether it's good enough. You don't daydream to please or impress anyone else. There are no standards to be met. You can let your daydreams flow freely without fear of judgement.

Daydreaming isn't outcome-based. You don't do it to produce or achieve anything. It isn't a means to an end. Once you're no longer using your daydreaming as an unhealthy coping mechanism, it becomes something you can do purely for fun. It becomes a form of play. And play is important, even for adults. As Brian Sutton-Smith said, "The opposite of play is not work, it's depression." Taking time to relax and do something purely for fun and not because it "advances" your life in some way is one way of protecting your mental health.

Your daydreaming is also a place where you can explore all those things that you'll never be able to do in real life. Do you want to have a picnic on Mars? Do you want to camp at the North Pole and watch the aurora? Do you want to stand on top of Everest? Is one life, no matter how fulfilling, just not *enough* for you? Your imagination can take you to all the places you want to go but realistically can't.

Daydreaming can also be useful

As a maladaptive daydreamer, you didn't allow yourself to see the positive aspects of your daydreaming. But as an immersive daydreamer, you can not only see the positives but you can also take them and make them work for you. Daydreaming no longer steals hours of your day, but you still have a way to pass the time when you're stuck in traffic. You can still dream about your ideal life, but now you can also work toward making it a reality. You can learn to manage your emotions in a healthy way, and your daydreaming and your characters can be a part of that. And you'll realize that sometimes controlled immersive daydreaming is healthier than falling into a negative spiral of worry or rumination.

Immersive daydreaming is different and beautiful

Being an immersive daydreamer isn't "normal". Your ability to create complex fictional scenarios in your head makes you different from most of the people around you. It's a difference that, as we've seen, isn't inherently a bad thing, provided you use it in a healthy way. It also doesn't have to be a difference that defines you. If you want, you could even choose not to daydream. That might be a tempting option if you're still living with the negative consequences of your maladaptive daydreaming. But it's possible that healthy immersive daydreaming could help you repair much of the damage.

Your daydreaming is, and always has been, the lens through which you view the world. It's why you think things through by imagining explaining them to someone else. It's why your mind is never still. It's why you can't imagine one object without generating the whole scene. It's why you're always wondering "what if –?" And none of that is bad or wrong. It simply is.

Once you stop constantly fighting your daydreaming and blaming it for your procrastination, once you stop seeing it as the cause of your other mental-health difficulties, you start to see all the wonderful things about being a daydreamer.

Immersive daydreaming isn't how most people think. Your mind does not work in a "typical" way. But it works in exactly the way that's right for you. And I hope that by the end of this book, you'll appreciate just how beautiful that is.

Worksheet: Shift your mindset

The worksheet that accompanies this chapter will help you stop focussing on the problems associated with being a maladaptive daydreamer and instead start to see the positives of being an immersive daydreamer.

Download the worksheet at:
https://daydreamplace.com/extreme-imagination/worksheet-chapter12.pdf

CHAPTER 13

RECONNECTING WITH YOUR AUTHENTIC SELF

As a maladaptive daydreamer, you might have lost your sense of self. It's understandable that you lose touch with who you are when you spend a lot of time imagining being someone else. But just as importantly, if you're using daydreaming to escape from a painful reality, you're also avoiding thinking about your real-life wishes and goals. You don't plan for the future. You wait for your life to unfold instead of steering it in the direction you want to go. And you let other people's expectations dictate what you do. You don't spend time getting to know yourself and understanding what's important to *you*.

If you're going to build a life you love, you need to know what that ideal life looks like. And that starts with knowing who you are and with reclaiming your authenticity. The good news is that, although your maladaptive daydreaming might have disconnected you from yourself, the person you become in your daydreams can help you find your way back.

Who is your daydream self?

If you daydream in first person, your daydream self is simply the person you become in your daydreams.

But what if you're not in your daydreams? What if you daydream in third person about a group of characters who aren't you? Or what if you have several different plots or daydream worlds and you become a different person in each of them?

In these cases, you might have to dig a little deeper to uncover your daydream self. If you daydream in third person, you might still have a main character. That main character could be your daydream self even though you don't view your daydream world through their eyes. They're your main character for a reason. If you feel more drawn to them than to your other characters, it could be because, at least subconsciously, you've poured a lot of yourself into them. Maybe their story is a way for you to express your hopes, dreams and aspirations. Maybe they're the person you would have liked to be.

Alternatively, if you become different people in different daydreams or you daydream in third person about a group of people, it could be that different aspects of your daydream self show up in different characters. Your daydream self could be a combination of several characters.

Whoever your daydream self is, the important thing to realize is that on some level they represent *you*. Not the version of you that you present to the real world, but the version of you that you are when you're free to be anyone you want. Your daydream self is a representation of your authentic self.

It's common to have a complicated relationship with your daydream self. They can feel like you and yet not like you at the same time. As Alice explained to me: "I have a daydream self. She's not exactly me. It's kind of complicated. She has two versions of herself. One's like the nicer version. And one's definitely a little unhinged. She represents me in a lot of ways. She has her own name, and she doesn't look exactly the same as me, but I know she's supposed to be me. But she's also a character, separate from me."

YOU CAN'T TAKE YOUR DAYDREAM SELF TOO LITERALLY

You might be reading this thinking, *"That's all well and good but what if my daydream self isn't me? What if they're a different gender or sexual orientation, for example? Does that mean I secretly want to adopt those traits in reality?"* Not necessarily. You can't take your daydreams that literally. The qualities of your daydream self that reveal who you are at your core are less perceptible than embodied characteristics such as gender. In your daydreams you might adopt certain characteristics simply because it allows you to take the plot in the direction you want it to go. Or you might want to explore what it would be like to live life from a different perspective.

For example, if you're female and you grew up in a family with traditional views on gender, you might have been told that good girls play quietly and don't cause any trouble. If your natural inclination was to be bold and loud and to confidently express your needs, that might have been met with disapproval. You might have suppressed your natural assertiveness in order to be more "acceptable". And if you got the idea that only boys were allowed to assert themselves, you might have become a boy in your daydreams – not because you identify as male but because daydreaming as a boy allowed you to freely express parts of yourself that you believed weren't appropriate in girls.

The point is, it's not the physical attributes of your daydream self that point the way to the real you. It's the values, motivations and personality traits that underlie your daydream self's outward appearance that you need to pay attention to, because even when you think your daydream self isn't you, there's probably a great deal of you in there.

YOUR IDEALIZED SELF

It's common for your daydream self to be a "better" version of you – smarter, funnier, more confident or more successful. They might have had more exciting opportunities, better friends or a life-changing stroke of luck. Instead of being you, they're the person you would have been if you could have chosen any life you wanted. That's called your idealized self.

There's nothing wrong with becoming an idealized version of yourself in your daydreams. It's not an unhealthy or worrying form of self-deception. In fact, it's showing you who you want to be. Your idealized self isn't like anyone else's idealized self. Your "perfect" life doesn't look like anyone else's "perfect" life. We all want different things. And what you want can tell you a lot about the person you are.

Everyone has different versions of themselves. We act differently in a business meeting from when we're out with our friends. We have a work persona, a family persona, a social persona, etc. It's normal to adapt who we are to the situation we're in, at least to a certain extent. In your daydream world, it's also natural to adapt yourself to fit your daydream situation. The difference is, in the real world we often adapt ourselves to meet other people's expectations. In your daydreams, the only person you have to please is you, so it's easier and safer than in real life to show up as your authentic self.

Why your daydream self can be real

You might think your daydream self is a figment of your imagination, just like the world they inhabit. After all, your characters are fictional creations. As we've seen, even if you base a character on a real person, they become fictional as soon as you put them in your daydream. But your daydream self is the exception. The most important thing I learned in overcoming my own maladaptive daydreaming is that my daydream self is the real me.

Maladaptive daydreamers spend a lot of time reminding themselves that their daydream world isn't real and that none of what goes on in their imagination is ever likely to happen in reality. And they assume that if nothing about their daydream world is real, their daydream self isn't real either.

There's a good reason why your daydream self is the exception to the rule that your characters aren't real. You can't put a real person in your daydreams, because you can't know how they'd think or act in any given situation. You don't know everything about them. So you have to fill in the gaps. But when it's you, you do know everything. Even if you put your daydream self in situations you've never faced in real life, you can still predict how you'd react.

WHERE ARE YOU MOST AUTHENTIC?

What qualities do you admire in your daydream self? Are they smart, confident, funny? Do they always know the right thing to say? Do they remain calm in the face of whatever challenge life throws at them? Those qualities are probably more present in you than you realize.

Was there a time when it wasn't safe for you to express those qualities in real life? Did you lose your confidence when someone laughed at you for reasons you didn't understand at the time? Did you hold back from saying what you thought because you were afraid of being judged? More often than not, the reason you can't express in reality the qualities that come so easily in your daydreams isn't that you don't have those qualities, but that life has taught you it's safer to suppress them. You might have suppressed them for so long that you don't even remember they're there. But they are, and in this chapter we'll see how you can bring them back to the surface.

We've all been shaped by the environment we grew up in and the things that happened to us. Real life has shaped you, and your daydream world has shaped your daydream self. There will be differences between you. But there will also be similarities. You and your daydream self will have some things in common. And the things you have in common are things that have survived the differences between your worlds. They're things that weren't determined by your circumstances. In other words, they're things that are a fundamental part of who you are. Your daydream self is a window to your authentic self.

WHO WOULD YOU BE IF YOU WERE FREE FROM ALL EXTERNAL CONSTRAINTS?

In the real world, we often suppress our true selves in order to fit in. We pretend to be someone we're not. We pretend to be the person we think the world wants us to be. Forming or maintaining connections with other people takes priority over being ourselves. We choose attachment over authenticity.

But in our daydreams, we're free to be whoever we like without fear of judgement or rejection. We can be the person we would have been if real life hadn't got in the way. We can be the person it isn't safe to be in the real world. In other words, we can be our authentic selves.

When you try to suppress a fundamental part of who you are, you don't destroy it. You shove it down somewhere deep where you hope the world won't see it. But the most genuine, authentic parts of you want to be seen. They *need* to be seen. So they come out in perhaps the only place they can: in your daydreams.

You need to rediscover your authentic self

Now that you understand why your daydream self could be closer to your authentic self than you realized, let's look at why it's so important to reconnect with your authentic self.

First, not being authentic in the real world can push you toward maladaptive daydreaming. It doesn't feel good to pretend to be someone you're not. It feels much better to be confidently and unapologetically yourself. And if the only place you can do that is in your daydreams, you're always going to be drawn back to them.

Second, being inauthentic makes it almost impossible to form meaningful social connections. How can you expect to connect deeply with someone when you don't allow them to see the truth of who you are? Many of us try to shape who we are in order to fit in and avoid rejection. But ironically, in so doing we bring about the very rejection we're trying to avoid. If someone is worth having in your life, they will like the authentic you much more than the fake version.

Third, when you aren't being your authentic self, you aren't living the life that was meant for you. You tend to go along with what other people want you to do. That might feel like the easiest option. But it isn't. Living a life that wasn't meant for you is hard and, ultimately, unfulfilling.

Your mental wellbeing depends on you living a life that's in alignment with the person you truly are. Not the person you've been showing up as until now, not the person your family or your culture wants you to be, but you. The real you. The person you are at your core.

If you don't like the person you are in the real world, pay attention. That's your subconscious sending you a message. You're uncomfortable with the way you're showing up in the world because you're getting it wrong. Not liking yourself is how your subconscious lets you know that you've become disconnected from your authentic self.

When you don't like yourself, you stop believing you're worthy of a better life. You don't set yourself big audacious goals. You stay small and you play small because you think that's all you deserve.

Just stop and think for a minute. Does your daydream self deserve a better life? Is your daydream self capable of creating that better life? Are they already creating it in the only place you're currently allowing them to – in your daydreams? If you answered yes to all those questions, isn't it time you gave your daydream self a chance to show you what they can do in the real world?

If you're going to build a happy and fulfilling life worthy of the beautiful soul you truly are, you have to do it as your authentic self. And if your authentic self is hiding in your daydreams, that means you're going to have to bring your daydream self into the real world.

How to reclaim your authenticity

It's easier than you think to bring your daydream self into the real world. By dropping the idea that your daydream self isn't real, you've already taken a huge step. The distance between your real-world self and your daydream self was being maintained, in part, by your belief that your daydream self isn't real. Once you see that your daydream self has more of you in them than you realized, it's much easier to bring aspects of your daydream self into the real world.

YOU'VE BEEN PRACTISING FOR A LONG TIME

In your daydreams, you've had a lot of practice being your daydream self. If they have a quality or trait that you admire, the chances are you have it too. You and your daydream self are separated only by external circumstances. The things you have in common are probably your fundamental strengths and values, and those are the things that count.

This isn't going to be a huge transformation. You aren't going to suddenly start showing up in the world as someone completely different. There's a good chance your friends and family won't even notice. You're just going to gradually start bringing the best aspects of your daydream self into your real life.

Whenever you're faced with a challenge or decision, ask yourself what your daydream self would do. Let your daydream self be your guide in every aspect of your life. You can use this technique to solve problems and make decisions. But you can also use it whenever you're tempted to be anything less than your best. When you feel like taking the easy way out, ask yourself whether your daydream self would do that. When you want to avoid something that feels scary, ask yourself whether your daydream self would run away. When you think you're not good enough or you're not worthy of something, ask yourself whether your daydream self deserves it.

When you're faced with a situation that makes you nervous, step into the persona of your daydream self for a minute and allow their capability and confidence to inspire you. Have fun pretending to be your daydream self for a while. You practise being them all the time when you're daydreaming, so it's easier than you think to be them in the real world too.

THE BENEFITS OF BEING MORE AUTHENTIC

As you get used to living as your daydream self, at least some of the time, you'll notice some important benefits. First, you'll have more confidence. Your daydream self will inspire you to get out of your comfort zone and test the limits of what you're capable of. And when you do that, you'll realize that you're capable of much more than you originally thought. Every challenge you overcome is evidence that you can step up to bigger challenges in the future. Your self-belief will be on an upward spiral.

Next, with that increasing confidence will come increased self-esteem. As you become more like your daydream self, you'll start to like yourself more. In part this comes from realizing you have more ability and potential than you thought. But it also comes from living more in alignment with who you really are. Deep down, you've always wanted to be your daydream self – that's why you made them who they are. Your daydream self is the person you were born to be and, if you allow it, the person you will inevitably become.

My journey back to myself

The importance of understanding who you become in your daydreams is something I've learned through personal experience. I would not be the person I am today if it were not for my daydream self. In fact, I wouldn't be alive today if it wasn't for my daydream self. My daydream self showed me how to heal from something that should have killed me.

I DISCONNECTED FROM MY TRUE SELF WHEN I WAS VERY YOUNG

For the first 49 years of my life, I was conscious of a disconnect between how the rest of the world saw me and how I saw myself. When I was young, the people around me saw a quiet, compliant, studious child. I saw a fiery, passionate free spirit who craved excitement and adventure. I don't know where the disconnect came from. Perhaps something traumatic happened to me when I was so young that I have no conscious memory of it. I don't know. It doesn't matter where it came from. All that matters is that it was there. And it was there from as far back as I can remember.

That disconnect was one of the reasons daydreaming was so compelling for me. In my daydreams, I could be myself. I could experience the adventure and excitement I craved. I didn't need to go thrill-seeking in the real world, because I could do whatever I wanted in my imagination. Realistically, the real world could never have measured up anyway.

But like all children, I was desperate to be accepted – by my family, my friends and everyone around me. And I believed that people expected me to show up in a certain way. So I tried to meet those expectations. I tried to be good, and quiet, and compliant because I thought that's what I had to do to be loved.

The more I showed up as that false version of me, the more convinced I became that that was who I had to be in order to be accepted, and the more determined I became to hide the real me. I suppressed my authentic self in everything I did. But thankfully my authentic self had my daydream world to hide in.

BEING DISCONNECTED FROM MYSELF MADE ME MISERABLE

I don't know how I lasted as long as I did. Even as an adult, everywhere I went, people saw a version of me that wasn't real. I hated the way I was showing up in real life. But I was too scared to break out of it. I was scared to disappoint people. I was scared of rejection.

And so I chose a life that allowed me to hide. In my career, I worked quietly behind the scenes, helping other people achieve their ambitions. But for my authentic self, it wasn't enough. I wanted *more* – more excitement, more recognition, more adventure. My real-world self didn't want or need to be seen, but my authentic self wasn't willing to blend quietly into the background.

Constantly suppressing my authentic self – constantly pretending to be someone I wasn't – took its toll. From the age of 18 until a couple of years ago, I had bouts of depression. Medication would take the edge off. CBT taught me strategies to mask the pain and appear functional. And then in March 2020, the world was plunged into the chaos and uncertainty of the Covid-19 pandemic.

LOCKDOWN AND BURNOUT

Lockdown affected everyone differently. For many daydreamers, it was the trigger for their daydreaming to become maladaptive. It's easy to see how being stuck at home with nothing to do, and coping with anxiety about when or if things would go back to normal, might push someone into excessive daydreaming. But for me it was the opposite. I was busier during lockdown than I'd ever been in my life.

I was trying to juggle a work-from-home job with home-schooling my youngest child, while failing to be a good-enough parent to two teenagers who had their own mental-health struggles. And I didn't have the time or the privacy to use my go-to coping mechanism, my daydreaming.

I nearly burned out during the first lockdown. When the UK went into the second lockdown, *every* working parent I knew struggled with their mental health, and I was no exception. By the time lockdown lifted, I was barely functioning. I thought with the end of the pandemic things would get better. But they didn't. A reorganization at work combined with family stress at home meant that there was always a crisis looming just around the corner. I kept telling myself that if I could make it through the next few weeks – get past the next bump in the road – everything would be OK. But I learned the hard way that you can't do that forever.

BREAKING POINT

I finally broke on 19 October 2021. I'd finished work the previous day with every intention of logging back in the next morning. I had projects I was working on and clients who were waiting for me to get back to them. But that Tuesday morning, I just couldn't do it anymore. Something in my head snapped. Everything felt overwhelming.

Over the following six days, I spiralled downward with terrifying speed. I became a ball of unbearable emotional pain, unable to stop the tears, unable to sleep, unable to eat; unable, even, to hug my husband and children, who had no idea how to help me.

In that place of desperation, I thought I had only one option. I needed to end my life. It was a sign of how broken I was that the idea of ending it all didn't feel sad or terrifying. It felt like the ultimate act of self-love. Life had asked more of me than I was capable of giving. And I'd gone along with it for far too long. I'd been trying to meet demands that were simply *too much*. I hadn't set boundaries. I hadn't said no. Because how do you say no to a job that you need? Or to children that you love? Or to lockdown rules that you have no control over? Every part of my life was non-negotiable, and so the only way I could say no was to say no to all of it. Ending my life was how I could take care of myself for what felt like the first time.

My husband got me admitted to a psychiatric hospital, which undoubtedly saved my life. I stayed there for a month. I received support, medication and therapy from people who seemed to genuinely care. Away from the demands of the outside world, life felt less desperate, less overwhelming. But it also felt empty – not depressing or meaningless, but literally empty. I didn't know who I was. I remembered everything about my life outside the hospital, and everything that had happened to me, but it no longer felt like my life. It was as if it had happened to someone else. The person I had been was just – gone. And that was a relief because deep down I knew I'd needed to shed my false self. I'd needed to release all the thoughts and behaviour patterns and coping mechanisms that hadn't been serving me. And when I hadn't taken charge and let those things go, something in my subconscious had done it for me. The false persona I'd clung on to all my life had, finally, died. I realized that the only way I was ever going to be mentally healthy, the only way I was ever going to be able to function in the real world, was to live in accordance with my values. I had to prioritize the things that mattered to me – in other words, I had to live as my authentic self.

HEALING

I worked through more than 200 hours of therapy in the first year after my mental-health crisis. If I hadn't been a daydreamer, it would have been a *lot* more. I was facing some huge challenges. First, I had to figure out who I was now that I wasn't the person I'd been before. Then, I had to figure out how to integrate that new person into the family I was determined to return to. And, finally, I had to decide what I wanted to do with the rest of my life. I was reinventing myself from nothing.

But every time I asked myself who I was becoming, the answer was right there. My daydream self. She'd been there all along, waiting to be set free. As soon as I let her, she showed me the way back to myself.

During my time in hospital, I realized that I had spent my whole life suppressing my authentic self because it felt safer to be the person that the people around me expected me to be. Fear of rejection had led me to reject myself. But my authentic self had been able to hide in the one place where she couldn't be rejected – my daydreams. My daydream self isn't the person I'd have liked to be, she's the person I was born to be. And once I accepted that, healing became much easier.

Worksheet: Getting to know the real you

In the worksheet that accompanies this chapter you'll answer questions as both your real-world self and your daydream self, and thereby get a clearer understanding of the ways in which you're similar. Don't skip this exercise if you don't have one obvious daydream self – analyzing some of your most important characters might still be helpful to you.

Download the worksheet at:
https://daydreamplace.com/extreme-imagination/worksheet-chapter13.pdf

CHAPTER 14

HOW YOUR CHARACTERS CAN SUPPORT YOU IN REAL LIFE

In this chapter, I'm going to introduce you to the concept of free characters. One of the beautiful things about being an immersive or maladaptive daydreamer is your ability to form real emotional connections with your characters. Those connections might have been what you were most afraid of losing as you overcame your maladaptive daydreaming. However, as we'll see in this chapter, as an immersive daydreamer you can build even deeper and more meaningful relationships with your characters *and* you can use those relationships to motivate and inspire you in the real world.

What is a free character?

Until now, we've talked about the people in your daydreams as daydream characters. They're like the characters in a book or TV show. They don't exist outside your plot. A free character is different. I call them free characters because they exist independently of any story you've put them in. They're "free" from your daydream world.

THE ILLUSION OF INDEPENDENT AGENCY
Many fiction writers experience something called "the illusion of independent agency" (Taylor et al., 2003). Characters they've created

in their imagination "come alive", and the author perceives them to be acting independently and dictating the direction and details of the plot. The same thing can happen with our daydream characters. Have you ever been surprised by something one of your characters did? Have you ever felt that they were pushing the story in a certain direction? That's the illusion of independent agency.

We get so used to thinking about how our characters would feel or act in any given situation that the process of deciding what they're going to do becomes automatic. We're no longer consciously aware of choosing how our character is going to behave, because our subconscious is now making those decisions. It feels to our conscious mind as though the character is acting independently.

I have the illusion of independent agency with two of my characters. And because their words and actions are chosen by my subconscious, these characters have become a window into my subconscious mind. In other words, they are the way I tap into my intuition.

HOW MY FREE CHARACTERS EVOLVED BEYOND THE DAYDREAM

I didn't create my free characters deliberately. Both of them showed up during moments of crisis. And I think there's a reason for that. When we're under extreme stress, it triggers our fight-or-flight response. Our mind has to assess the threat and decide on the best way to respond to it. Sometimes, the best response is to remain focussed firmly on the present moment, alert to danger. If your mind has decided you need to stay present, you're not going to be able to escape into a daydream. Many daydreamers find that they can't get into their daydream world in moments of extreme stress. Their go-to coping mechanism deserts them when they need it most. When that happened to me, my mind needed to simultaneously stay present in reality *and* seek support and comfort from my daydream character. And so my mind released my character from the daydream world and allowed me to imagine interacting with them in real life.

Connected daydreaming

When you take a character out of your daydream world and start talking to them about your real life, they go from being a daydream character to a free character. I call talking to your free characters about real life "connected daydreaming". It's connected because it *connects* your real life and your daydreams. Disappearing into your daydream world, particularly if you're a maladaptive daydreamer, is an escape. It's a way to avoid real life. But connected daydreaming allows you to confront real life head-on. It allows you to use your imagination while staying grounded in reality.

Connected daydreaming takes place *outside* your daydream world. The events in your daydream world aren't real when you're engaged in connected daydreaming. And one consequence of that is you have to daydream as your real-world self, not your daydream self. It has to be your real-world self that shows up when you're discussing real life. The things you talk to your free characters about need to be incorporated into your connected daydreaming exactly as they are in reality – no editing, no rewriting history, no fantasizing about an unrealistic future.

Connected daydreaming is probably something you avoided as a maladaptive daydreamer because you were worried it might make you even more mentally unwell than you already thought you were. But, in fact, connected daydreaming can be a powerful way to increase your confidence and motivation and boost your mental wellbeing.

Connected daydreaming lies in between immersive daydreaming and mind-wandering. It's focussed, deliberate and stays on one topic like immersive daydreaming. But it's connected to your real life in a way that's more like mind-wandering. And like mind-wandering, it can help you solve problems and make sense of the world.

TALKING TO YOUR DAYDREAM SELF

If you're not comfortable with creating a free character, you could instead cultivate a relationship with your daydream self. As we saw in Chapter 13, your daydream self probably represents aspects of your authentic self. Learning to talk to your daydream self through connected daydreaming can help you to bring your authentic self into the real world. When you're facing a challenging situation, you can ask your daydream self to guide you. You can form a partnership and tackle the challenge together.

If your daydream self suggests something that feels unrealistic to your real-world self, explore that with them. Tell them why you can't do it and ask them why they think you can. This kind of dialogue can help you see past your limitations. You might find that the solution you instinctively thought was out of reach is merely out of your comfort zone and not so unachievable after all.

MAKING CONNECTED DAYDREAMING A DAILY HABIT

In the worksheet that accompanies this chapter, I explain how to create a free character and start talking to them through connected daydreaming. I recommend making time every day to connect with your free character(s). It's daydreaming time, but not in an escapist or avoidant way. It's daydreaming with a purpose. You talk to your free character about your real life. You tell them what's happening, what's going well, what isn't going so well. If you're struggling with a problem or decision, you talk it over with them and ask their advice. It feels similar to a conversation with a trusted friend.

If you have allocated time for daydreaming, you could experiment with using part of that time for connected daydreaming and see what effect it has on your self-esteem, your motivation and your ability to take action on your goals.

I try to go for a walk with one of my free characters every day. It's a key part of how I manage my mental health. I always come back from our walks feeling calm and peaceful but also motivated and inspired. And it's during the conversations with my free character that I have most of my creative ideas, figure out solutions to my problems and release any unhelpful emotions or thinking patterns.

Talking a problem over with someone you trust can help you see a situation from a different perspective, get valuable advice and perhaps see a way forward that you hadn't considered before. Connected daydreaming gives you many of the same benefits. Instead of talking to another person, you're talking to your subconscious mind in the form of your free character. Sometimes that means the perspective isn't as different as it would be if you were talking to someone real. But that's counterbalanced by the fact that ideas that come from your subconscious mind are likely to be more in tune with what feels authentic for you.

Your free characters can also gently hold you accountable when you're working on improving your life. You can discuss your goals and your progress with them, and you can use the genuine emotional attachment you have to them to your advantage. Because you don't want to let them down. When my self-esteem was close to non-existent, I would give up on my goals all too easily because I didn't think I was worthy of the achievement. But my free characters knew what my daydream self – my authentic self – was capable of. And they weren't going to accept anything less from the real-world me. When I doubted myself, they had faith in me. And when I didn't mind letting myself down, I would still do anything to avoid disappointing them.

Chet's story

Chet has several free characters that help him make decisions on a daily basis. He told me this story as an example of how one of his characters, Coach, acts as his conscience. Coach encourages him to do the right thing when he's engaging in self-sabotaging behaviours. It's a great example of how we might listen to the advice of a free character when we're resisting making a responsible choice.

"It's 11 p.m. I'd resolved to go to bed at 10 p.m., so already I'm late for bed. This has never stopped me before, however, since Netflix has never expressed any disapproval of me watching movies past bedtime.

"The part of me that knows what's best for me gives me a generally undesired slap in the face; I name this character 'Coach'. Coach bursts out at me in reaction to my irresponsible Netflix watching: '*What the hell are you doing?*'

"'Coach! Didn't see – er, think – you there! Uh, what the heck are you talking about?' I imagine myself saying, nervously trying to figure a way I can hide what I'm doing from a character in my own brain.

"There's a bit of silence clearly denoting Coach's unconditional scorn at my futile weaselling. He forms his next words very slowly.

"'Need . . . I . . . remind you . . . that tomorrow is the last . . . day . . . to pay this month's rent. If you don't write and deliver a cheque by 5 p.m. to the rental office, you'll be in danger of eviction! And you won't even be up at 5 p.m., anyway, if you stay up for 12 hours watching Netflix, then fall into hibernation for the next decade from complete fatigue!'

"Meanwhile, on Netflix, my newest favourite superhero is casting powerful lightning bolts at my new favourite show's primary villain.

"'Coach, are you seeing this!? I haven't seen a battle this epic since my ten-hour binging of my previous favourite show last night!'

"Another beat of silence signifying Coach's continued scorn. No actual words are necessary.

"'Fine!' I say aloud, as I grab a piece of paper and a Sharpie and scribble 'PAY RENT BY 5 P.M.' in incoherent handwriting. I crumple it up and toss it behind me, vaguely in the direction of my bed.

"I continue watching my show.

"Coach clears his throat in continued tacit scorn, silently judging the complete inability of the tossed crumpled note to alter my behaviour.

"'Fine, damn you!' I yell, then pause my show. I scour my messy room for where I last threw my alarm clock, find it, and relocate it back by my bed where Coach thinks it belongs. I set the alarm for 4.45 p.m., clearly enough time to get dressed, write a cheque, and walk down to the rental office. 'Happy?' I say aloud.

"'Let's pretend for a moment that you've covered the rent-payment task with flying colours—'

"'Yes, I'm very good at pretending. I created you, didn't I?'

"Coach sighs. 'Look, can you at least resolve to go outside tomorrow and see some real people? I hate you sitting around watching TV all day cooped up inside.'

"I pause Netflix, AGAIN. I sigh, grab another piece of paper, and write 'BRING DOUGHNUTS TO OFFICE STAFF PEOPLE WHEN PAY RENT' on a note that I tape just above my alarm clock.

"'Happy? I swear to be friendly with the office staff when I pay the rent, tomorrow. I'll bring them doughnuts and be very nice, asking how their day is going, and what they think their dogs or kids or whatever are getting away with at home while they're at work. OK?'

"'Tolerably close, but no cigar. Fifteen minutes isn't nearly enough time to buy doughnuts, let alone strike up a conversation once you're at the office. Now we're back at potential eviction territory, which we haven't even strayed that far away from to begin with!'

"I finally give in as much as is mentally possible for me. I change my alarm from 4.45 to 3 p.m., a benevolent two hours before the rent duetime. All this resolved, I begrudgingly watch Netflix for only another 20 minutes, as opposed to the five or more hours I'd keep watching if I ever got my own way. I shut off the light and go to bed by midnight."

We've all been in situations similar to Chet's, where we've been procrastinating about doing something. When your conscience is trying to get you to be responsible, if you push it down and ignore it, you're likely to continue with whatever activity you're using to procrastinate. In Chet's case, he could have continued watching TV as a way to ignore the fact that his rent was due. But by visualizing his conscience as Coach, he was able to listen to what Coach had to say. And he was able to reach a compromise where he watched TV for a further 20 minutes and then went to bed at a time that would allow him to get up early enough to pay his rent the following day.

Why connected daydreaming is helpful

There are many ways connected daydreaming can help you improve yourself and your life, such as:

- Your free character lives in your subconscious mind. They know *everything* about you, including what you're capable of. They see your authentic self and the person you have the potential to become. They see possibilities that you might have kept hidden from your real-world friends and family. They view the real-world you as someone who is becoming the daydream version of you that they have known and loved all along.

- Your relationship with your free character is safe and secure. You can practise showing up as your authentic self with them because there's no judgement. And your conversations can go deep. When you feel totally safe with someone, you can let them into the deepest corners of your soul. You can share your greatest fears. You can be vulnerable. And that sets the stage for some truly life-changing conversations.

- Your free character can give you surprisingly good advice. Remember, they represent your intuition, which can be a powerful force if you let it. And you might find you don't resist the advice of your free character the way you would if anyone else tried to tell you what to do.

- Your free character can bring love, connection and a sense of belonging into your life. The emotions you feel toward them are real. And the emotions you feel *from* them are real too. It doesn't matter that the character isn't real. When you allow the love that your character has for you to light up your soul, you're able to be more loving toward the people around you in the real world.

- Your free character can teach you to love yourself. When your free character tells you that you're amazing, or lovable, or talented, it's easier to believe than if you just try to tell yourself that. And when your free character tells you that you're capable of doing something, they say it with conviction and total faith in you. You can find the courage to try new things, because you know your free character will celebrate with you if it works out and offer emotional support if it doesn't.

- Your free character is always available. They're just a thought away. You can talk to them whenever you need to. It doesn't matter if you need a long conversation or a quick check-in; they're there for you.

- Your relationship with your free character is all about you. It's like having a personal therapist. All your conversations are focussed on *your* life.

AN ANTIDOTE TO YOUR INNER CRITIC

Your inner critic is the voice inside your head that points out everything you've done wrong, tells you that you aren't good enough and is convinced that nobody likes you. We all have one. And for the most part, your inner critic is trying to keep you safe. It's trying to protect you by stopping you from taking risks. Your inner critic tells you it's safer not to try, because if you don't try, you can't fail.

But, of course, if you don't try, you also can't succeed. To live life to the full and become the best possible version of yourself, you have to tame your inner critic. And connected daydreaming can help you do that, because your free character can be a powerful antidote to your inner critic.

CBT recommends challenging the inner critic. When your inner critic says something negative, you should immediately counteract that thought with a more realistic or positive alternative. But if you've ever tried to argue with your inner critic by telling yourself that you *are* good enough, you *are* worthy, you *are* capable, you've probably found it's not that easy. Because if you don't believe it – and most of us don't – then those positive affirmations are just words.

However, your free character *does* believe that more positive alternative. Your free character *does* think you're talented and lovable – even when your inner critic is saying the opposite. Once you get used to talking to your free character, you might find they automatically argue with your inner critic on your behalf.

Having a secure relationship with your free character can give you the confidence to try new things and push yourself out of your comfort zone. What normally keeps us in our comfort zone is fear of failure. But when you know your free character will love you even if you fail, the possibility of failure doesn't seem so scary after all.

HOW MY FREE CHARACTERS SAVED MY LIFE

When I had my mental-health crisis in the autumn of 2021, it was the love I felt from my two free characters that got me through it. Being suicidal wasn't anything like I'd imagined. I didn't want to die, but I didn't believe I had the strength to go on living. And no one outside of me could have convinced me otherwise. No one outside of me knew how exhausted I was or what it was going to take to pull myself out of the huge hole I was in. But my two free characters knew. They *knew* how hard it was going to be, and they also *knew* that I was strong enough to do it. I didn't agree with them, but I did trust them. They love me unconditionally. If I hadn't believed that love was real, and if I hadn't accepted that they knew me better than I knew myself, I'd be dead. But because of them, I accepted the support that was being offered to me. I went into hospital. I engaged with therapy. And, with the support of my free characters, I dragged myself out of the darkness.

It's because of one of my free characters that this book exists. Shortly before I left hospital, I asked him, "*What am I supposed to do with the rest of my life?*" The answer came back: "*You are a writer. You have always been a writer. You just need to start writing.*" And when I was well enough, that's exactly what I did.

Worksheet: Meeting your free character

The worksheet that accompanies this chapter will walk you step by step through the process of bringing one of your characters out of your daydream world so that they can become your most powerful supporter in real life.

Download the worksheet at:
https://daydreamplace.com/extreme-imagination/worksheet-chapter14.pdf

CHAPTER 15

USE YOUR DAYDREAMING TO TRANSFORM YOUR LIFE

In this chapter, we're going to look at how you can use your daydreaming to enhance your everyday life. In Chapters 13 and 14, we looked at how your daydream self can help you discover your authentic self and how your daydream characters can support you in real life. Now we're going to look at little things you can do every day to make the most of the incredible gift that is immersive daydreaming.

Managing negative emotions

Immersive daydreaming becomes maladaptive when you use it to run away from difficult emotions. But once you have control over your daydreaming, you can use it in an intentional way to help you with emotional regulation. This differs from daydreaming to escape from negative emotions in three important ways. First, you're doing it deliberately because you've made a conscious decision that it's appropriate in that moment; it's not an automatic reaction. Second, you're daydreaming only for as long as necessary. And third, your daydream helps you to process a negative emotion instead of avoiding it, so you feel better after, as well as during, the daydream.

You can use your daydreaming to process an emotion that it isn't safe or appropriate to express in the real world. For example, if something at work made you angry, it might not be helpful to yell at your boss, even if that's what you feel like doing. So you suppress your anger and respond politely. But the anger still has to go somewhere. Daydreaming one brief scene where your daydream self gets justifiably angry and expresses it can help you to release your real-life anger.

You can also use a brief daydream to snap yourself out of an unhelpful spiral of worry or rumination. When you're obsessing over negative thoughts, it can be helpful to shift your mind off that topic completely with a brief daydream so that you can come back to reality in a different place. For example, when you're worried about something bad that could happen, you might find yourself turning it over and over in your mind, trying to plan for every possible outcome. Telling yourself to stop thinking about it doesn't work. But if you set a timer for five minutes and allow yourself to sink into a comforting or uplifting daydream, you might find that when you come back to reality, your thoughts turn to something different, such as how you're going to spend the rest of the day. The brief daydream serves as a mental reset that breaks the spiral of worry or rumination.

Another way that you can use your daydreaming to process difficult emotions is by leaning on one of your characters for support. You could do this directly through connected daydreaming, as we discussed in Chapter 14. Or you can create similar emotions in your daydream world and work through them there. Alice explained to me how she does this.

ALICE'S EMOTIONAL-SUPPORT CHARACTER

Alice created a daydream character when she was 16. At first, he was a cool musician. But as Alice's mental health deteriorated, her character evolved to meet her changing emotional needs. He became her source of emotional support and the person she could turn to when she needed to talk. Alice's story vividly captures the beauty and depth that can be found in a daydream relationship.

"When I was 16, I moved out of my family's house and into a boarding programme at our school. During that time, my daydreaming changed drastically. It got intense, like very intense. I was completely addicted to this one character I created. Every time I thought about him, any daydream I had with him, it was just so addictive. He literally was like a drug to me. He was like electricity. I would come home from school and go to my dorm room and just daydream."

I asked Alice if she had based this character on anyone she knew.

"He's completely made up. He was influenced by a couple of musicians that I liked at the time and probably also other people, but he was himself. He wasn't based on anyone in my day-to-day life."

"Does the fact he isn't real affect how you feel about him?" I asked.

Alice paused to think. I could tell that she was finding it hard to put her feelings into words.

"He is very attractive to me. He could be my ideal man. But I think part of what makes him so awesome to me is the fact that we're connected in a way that we wouldn't be if he was a real person. I think with real people, I have this fear that I'll never be close enough. Connections with people are sometimes not deep enough, not intense enough, not intimate enough, not powerful enough for me. So I find that with my daydream characters."

I asked her how long this character has been in her daydreams.

"I'm 22 now, so six years. There was a period of maybe a year where he wasn't really in my daydreams, because I created a new daydream. But now he's back. I'm different, he's a little bit different."

"How is he different?" I asked.

"I often daydream to think about certain things. A lot of times currently it's mental health and mental illnesses. So, he's changed in the sense that what I want him to represent has changed. When I was a teenager, he was just this musician. Now our daydreams together are more like he's with me in this mental illness thing. We're both older, and time and bad friendships and relationships have taken their toll on both of us. So whenever I would have a crush on someone that didn't work out, or a falling out with a friend, I would have him go through something parallel to that, so that it made sense that he would feel the same way that I did, but as himself."

I think this is the lovely thing about a daydream relationship. In real life, your friends and family are leading their own lives, having experiences that are different from yours, and they can't always relate to everything you're going through. Over time, if their life goes in a different direction, your connection with them might fade away. But as Alice's life changes, her character goes through parallel experiences. He evolves in the same direction she does. So Alice knows that no matter what life throws at her, her character will always understand how she feels.

Alice has several other characters who have also become important to her. I asked her to sum up what it means to have them in her life.

"I think it's really incredible. We are sort of a family. They get the deepest parts of me, and, in a way, they protect me. Not literally, but emotionally. I don't feel like I can be myself or express my emotions in the real world, so I have this protective group of people in my head. I know they've got me no matter what. And that's something that I'm really thankful for."

DAYDREAMING AFTER A MISTAKE OR ARGUMENT

One way I use my ability to daydream is when I've acted impulsively and done something I regret. If I've unintentionally upset someone, I feel an overwhelming urge to fix it *right now*. But I've learned over the years that some things are best left to settle. Trying to resolve an argument when both parties are still feeling emotional, or trying to repair a mistake before fully understanding the consequences of it, can often make things worse.

My urge to fix things right now comes from my inability to tolerate the stress of knowing I messed up. I find it difficult to sit with the discomfort of knowing that someone's upset with me. But I've learned to use my daydreaming to manage conflict and repair mistakes in a calmer and more constructive way.

First, I'll use daydreaming as a distraction. If I've had an argument with someone and we both need time to calm down, daydreaming allows me to escape the discomfort of the unresolved situation. I can come back to reality a little later, feeling calmer and knowing that the other person has had time to get their thoughts and feelings in order.

Next, if my emotions are preventing me from resolving something, I can use an appropriate scene from my daydream plot to feel and process those emotions in a safe way that won't escalate the real-life situation.

I might also discuss what's happened with one of my free characters. That gives me a bit of distance from the situation and helps me put things in perspective. By getting out of my own head and listening to my character's advice, I can often see the situation more objectively, without my heightened emotions getting in the way.

Another useful technique is to use my daydreaming to put me in a more compassionate frame of mind. I might daydream a scene where I feel deeply and lovingly connected to one of my characters. And I gather up all that love and hold on to it. So when I return to the real world, I'm able to act more lovingly toward those around me.

Finally, if I need to have a difficult conversation with someone to resolve whatever has happened, I'll run through that conversation in a daydream beforehand. But I'm not rehearsing the conversation the way I think it will go or the way I fear it might go; I'm rehearsing it the way I want it to go. I daydream a version of the conversation in which the other person apologizes for what they did wrong and forgives me for what I did wrong. I daydream that we put the argument behind us and become friends again. *It doesn't matter if this daydream isn't entirely realistic,* because it's not just a rehearsal. I'm repairing the relationship in my mind. I'm letting go of any anger or resentment I feel toward the other person. And that allows me to approach the real conversation from a place of compassion. When you can enter a difficult conversation with compassion and empathy, you're much more likely to get the outcome you want.

To deal with one argument or mistake, I might use several different daydreaming techniques. But all of them help me to resolve the situation in a calm and constructive way. This is a powerful example of how you can make your daydreaming work in your favour once you stop using it merely to run away from difficult situations.

Daydreaming to evoke positive emotions

In addition to using daydreaming to manage negative emotions, you can use daydreaming to give yourself a quick boost of positivity whenever you need it. This works because we can feel real emotions in response to things that exist only in our imagination. The fact that the emotions are real, even when the events and characters aren't, is one of the things that made maladaptive daydreaming so compelling, but it's also something you can use to your advantage.

You can build up a library of scenes that you can use to evoke positive emotions whenever you need them. These are little micro-daydreams that last a few seconds to a minute at most. The scenes don't change over time, so they're not somewhere that you work through your problems. Their only purpose is to evoke a flood of positive emotions.

The important thing is that these scenes are *short*, so be careful with this if your maladaptive daydreaming still isn't fully under control. If you use scenes from your normal daydream world, choose ones that are stable and have a definite end point so you're not tempted to stay and explore what happens next. Alternatively, you could create scenes purely in order to generate specific emotions and not connect them to your daydream world at all.

For example, to generate a feeling of calm, you might imagine relaxing outside on a warm summer's evening, watching the sun set, with your daydream partner beside you. To generate confidence, you might imagine a victory scene where your characters are in awe of your daydream self's courage and talent. And when you want to feel validated, you might imagine one of your characters listening compassionately to you and understanding exactly how you feel.

Having a set of go-to short scenes allows you to take a mental reset whenever you're feeling discouraged or overwhelmed. You zone out for just a few seconds, generate the emotions you need and then go on with your day in a more positive frame of mind.

Life rarely gives us all the emotions we need on a daily basis. It's perfectly normal to have days when you don't feel as much love or connection as you'd like or when moments of calm are few and far between. And on those days, having a quick way to generate positive emotions can be invaluable.

Daydreaming to increase your confidence

You can extend this idea of micro-daydreaming to deliberately generate the optimal mindset for whatever situation you're in. For example, if you're about to give a presentation at work and you're nervous about it, one way to use your daydreaming would be to imagine giving the presentation and having it all go perfectly. You could imagine every detail of the presentation as if you're mentally rehearsing it. That might help you feel more prepared. But you might find it difficult to picture yourself confidently giving the presentation, because you know you don't feel that confident.

If that's the case, you can be a little more creative. You can daydream *any* scene from your plot where you feel supremely confident and achieve something awesome. It doesn't have to be realistic, because it's not a mental rehearsal. What you take from the daydream is how it makes you *feel*. Find a scene where you *feel* confident about tackling the huge challenge in front of you. Run that scene, and savour all of the positive emotions it brings up. Then hang on to those emotions when you come back to the real world. Take that confidence and positivity into the real-life situation and notice how you're able to show up differently.

Manifesting and the Law of Attraction

If you're active on social media, you've probably seen people talking about manifesting and the Law of Attraction. You might also have seen it referred to as Lucky Girl Syndrome. The idea is that you can shape your reality by aligning your thoughts and feelings with the vibration of whatever you want to manifest. But if you've ever daydreamed about something you hoped would happen in real life, you're probably painfully aware that thinking about something – even for several hours a day – isn't enough to magically make it happen. Does that mean that manifesting doesn't work? Is the Law of Attraction just a myth?

DAYDREAMING ISN'T MANIFESTING

I have personally experienced the power of manifestation. But nothing I've daydreamed about has ever happened in exactly the way I imagined it, because daydreaming isn't manifesting. Manifesting relies on the idea that you attract what you want by becoming a vibrational match for it. In practical terms, that means you have to *believe* that what you're trying to manifest is going to happen. That's the crucial difference between daydreaming and manifesting.

In immersive and maladaptive daydreaming *we know our fantasies aren't real*. That's probably something you kept reminding yourself of when your maladaptive daydreaming was at its worst. It was reassuring that you could still tell the difference between fantasy and reality, right? But manifesting relies on you blurring that distinction. When you're manifesting, you have to believe that what you want will be real before it is real. Manifesting involves *expectation*. Daydreaming, on the other hand, involves *hope*. They're completely different things.

If you daydream as an idealized version of yourself, you have a further problem. When you're daydreaming, you're not manifesting for you. At best, you're manifesting for your daydream self. It's not going to translate into the real world, because you're not that person in the real world.

Finally, to manifest, you have to align yourself with the life you want. That means you have to be able to live, right now, with the mindset of the person you will be after you've successfully manifested what you want. And therefore you have to believe you *deserve* the thing you're manifesting. If you lived with crippling shame when you were a maladaptive daydreamer, you probably didn't believe you deserved *anything*, least of all that perfect life you were daydreaming about. It's not surprising that you never manifested it.

MANIFESTING INVOLVES MORE THAN JUST THOUGHTS

As we've seen, daydreaming often prevents us from taking action. Daydreaming about something is more fun than exercising the discipline and patience required to make that daydream a reality. But there's more to manifesting than just visualizing what you want.

You have to take action as well. That's the part nobody talks about, because it isn't sexy, or fun, or easy. But it is necessary. The universe does not magically give you something just because you wish for it.

The power of manifesting lies in the mindset shift that occurs when you believe that you deserve, and will get, the thing you want. Visualizing what you want doesn't mean you don't have to do the work to get it. But it does make it easier to do that work. When you believe that something is already in your future, taking the necessary action feels like a natural part of the process. You're excited about doing the work because you *know* that your reward is coming. Aligning your mindset with the end result *also* aligns your mindset with the actions you need to take.

MY EXPERIENCE OF MANIFESTING

Manifesting requires total dedication and self-belief, and I've only committed to the process once: during my second pregnancy. With my first pregnancy, I'd had few choices over how I gave birth. Twin pregnancies are automatically considered high-risk, and so I had to give birth under controlled and medicalized conditions. Everything went smoothly, the staff were fantastic and my daughters were delivered safely. Finally becoming a parent after a six-year battle with infertility was a dream come true. But the birth itself wasn't much fun, so the second time around I wanted to do things differently.

I'd always wanted a water birth. So when I became pregnant for the second time, that became my goal. I had a beautiful vision of giving birth calmly and easily in a warm birthing pool with my husband beside me, soft music playing in the background and maybe even a few candles. I daydreamed about that birth for months.

But there was a problem. In a water birth, your options for pain relief are limited. Giving birth to my twins had hurt. I'd accepted every form of pain relief offered to me, including an epidural, which wouldn't be possible in the birthing pool. If I was going to have a water birth, I had to find a way to make it less painful than last time.

I read everything I could find about natural childbirth. I went to pregnancy yoga classes. I listened to hypnosis recordings. In other words, I took action. I made sure that my mind and body were as prepared as they possibly could be for an easy and natural birth. And, crucially, I *believed* that I was going to have a good birth.

The belief and the action went hand in hand. The midwife had told me there was no medical reason I couldn't have a water birth, and I was doing everything I could to prepare for one. Knowing that I was doing everything I could helped me to believe that it would happen. And believing it was going to happen motivated me to prepare for it.

But, as sometimes happens with manifesting, things didn't unfold the way I'd imagined. I daydreamed about that water birth every day for almost the whole nine months. But what I was actually preparing for was an easy and relatively pain-free birth. When I started having contractions at 7 p.m. on a Thursday, I didn't think I was in labour. The contractions weren't that painful – even though they were only four minutes apart. I phoned the midwife, who advised me to go in and get checked out but told me not to hurry. I'm glad I didn't. My son was born calmly and easily on the bathroom floor 50 minutes later, with just my husband, a close friend and a nervous-looking paramedic in attendance. I didn't get my water birth. I never even got to the birthing centre. But it didn't matter. Giving birth to my son was the most beautiful and empowering experience of my life. I'd put in the work, and I got my wish – albeit in a way that looked *nothing* like my daydream.

DAYDREAMERS CAN BE GREAT MANIFESTORS

What my experience taught me is that daydreamers can learn to manifest, and we can be great at it. But if we're not intentional about what we're doing, we're likely to get it wrong and repel rather than attract the thing we're daydreaming about.

To manifest successfully as a daydreamer, you have to be clear about what you want. You have to visualize your dream in enough detail that it feels real to you. And then you have to allow yourself to *believe* that you can make it real. You have to let your vision inspire you. And then you have to follow through and take the necessary action. You have to believe not just in the reality of your imagined future but in your ability to create it. The purpose of your vision isn't to show you the future, it's to show you the way. Your dream might come true in a way that's different from what you originally visualized. But if you've done the work, what you get will be every bit as rewarding as what you imagined.

The place of peace

Something I've personally found helpful is what I call a "place of peace". This is an imaginary safe space that I can go to whenever I need to step away from reality. It's somewhere I can think clearly, see the bigger picture and let intense emotions subside.

It's worth taking some time to create a place of peace. What you choose to create will be personal to you. It could be based on a real place where you feel (or remember feeling) safe and happy, or it could be somewhere that exists only in your imagination. A natural setting, such as a beach or forest, works well. But you could go for something more fantastical if you like – you could imagine being inside a warm fluffy white cloud, or floating out in the ocean miles from anywhere. You might prefer to imagine a cosy log cabin or a temple filled with items of significance to you. The possibilities are endless.

My place of peace is an English woodland. It's based on a real place I know well. As soon as I close my eyes, I can picture the path through the trees. It's springtime, the bluebells are out and their scent fills the air. I can hear birds singing in the trees, and the occasional tap-tap-tap of a woodpecker. The path is soft, almost muddy in places, and comfortable to walk along. There's a fallen tree at the side of the path. Sometimes I'll climb up onto it and sit for a minute. And when I'm there, I feel as though I've come home.

That's the feeling you're aiming for. A feeling of familiarity, safety and belonging. I recommend spending a few minutes every day vividly imagining your place of peace and tuning into the positive emotions it generates. You want to become so familiar with this place that you can be there in an instant.

Once you can get to your place of peace easily and naturally, you can start to use it for emotional regulation. When something upsetting happens or your emotions threaten to spiral out of control, you can stop, close your eyes, take one deep breath and immediately be somewhere safe and comforting.

Sometimes, that's all you need. Spending a minute or two in your place of peace can allow intense emotions to pass, and you can return to reality feeling calmer and more rational. Once you've created your place of peace, you can also use it as the basis for your own personal meditation.

USING YOUR PLACE OF PEACE IN MEDITATION

You can combine the benefits of mindfulness that we discussed in Chapter 9 with the benefits of creating a free character that we discussed in Chapter 14 by meeting your free character in your place of peace as part of your own personalized meditation.

You start by taking a few deep, relaxing breaths, as you would at the beginning of any meditation, and then you imagine yourself in your place of peace. Once you're feeling calm and comfortable, imagine one of your free characters joining you. And then simply imagine talking to them about what's going on in real life. Don't be afraid to feel your emotions. This is a safe space where you can be angry or sad. You can cry if you need to. You know your free character won't judge you. They're there to support and comfort you.

Sometimes, having a good cry and letting your free character hug you will be all you need. At other times, you might choose to use your place of peace as a doorway into your subconscious mind. To do this, you can ask your free character for advice. Then you quiet your mind as best you can and listen for the answer. More often than not, your free character will tell you something insightful that your conscious mind wouldn't have thought of.

You can prevent your place of peace from being a gateway to uncontrolled daydreaming by keeping it simple. It should be *one* place, *one* scene. By not allowing that scene to build into an entire story, you'll find it easier to keep your imagination under control. And talking to your free character about real life while you're there will help you stay grounded too.

I've been using my place of peace for over a decade now. I've used it to manage anxiety while waiting for appointments and to zone out while at the dentist. And the conversations I've had with my daydream mentor in that place have helped me find my way through countless challenging situations.

Sola's story

As you've seen, your daydreams can act as a window into your subconscious mind. This can help you reconnect with your authentic self, and you can even talk to your subconscious through a free character. Sola has taken this a step further. She has found that by analyzing the themes in her daydreams, she's been able to understand herself better, boost her confidence and get clarity on what's most important to her. She gave me an example of how analyzing what she's daydreaming about helps her in the real world.

"A few weeks back I had a blast of a time with these people I had just met. And the next day, I kept having daydreams about them, of us partnering up together in my current project, or having a Christmas party together. And now I will see the daydream objectively. So I will pause and say '*I see that you're having these daydreams where you are connecting more with those friends you met yesterday*' and I would acknowledge my desires. This is hugely powerful. I will accept the fact that I have the desire to connect with more people and I might actually have the ability to do that. I call this 'daydream portal'. This is where all my daydreams are coming from. And when the daydream portal keeps showing me these daydreams, although it might not exactly be the reality, it's giving me the idea that when the time and place are not limited, this is something I'm capable of.

"So I remember last week I was trying to focus, but the daydream was just loud, and it was not going away. I kept shoving it down, but it didn't go. When that happens, what I do is let myself daydream for just five minutes or ten minutes. Because my daydream portal is trying to tell me something. So I take a bit of time to listen to it, maybe go for a walk."

I think working with your daydreaming in this way allows you to become aware of what's possible. You can listen to your subconscious and the messages it's trying to send you. Sola feels that her relationship with her daydreaming improved after she learned to accept herself as a daydreamer.

"This is why self-love is so important. You no longer use daydreams to avoid reality but as something you communicate with to design the life you deeply desire. The more you are aware of your daydreams and learn to love and accept what they are telling you, the more you will learn about yourself. I can't imagine living my life without my daydreams now. Daydreaming is a magical way to process my thoughts and emotions, a mirror of my desires, and something that I keep a keen eye on to envision my next step in life."

Sola's story is a beautiful illustration of the transformation that's possible when you release any shame you feel about being a daydreamer and learn to love both yourself and your daydreaming.

Worksheet: Unleash your creativity

The worksheet that accompanies this chapter is a brainstorming exercise that invites you to get creative about how you could use your talents as an immersive daydreamer to improve your life.

Download the worksheet at:
https://daydreamplace.com/extreme-imagination/worksheet-chapter15.pdf

CHAPTER 16

FINAL THOUGHTS

My goal in writing this book was to summarize everything I've learned about immersive and maladaptive daydreaming so that you can learn in a few weeks what took me years to figure out. If you're finishing this book with a better understanding of what immersive and maladaptive daydreaming are, and if you're well on the way to turning your maladaptive daydreaming into the beautiful immersive daydreaming it was always meant to be, then I've done my job. Where you go from here is up to you. You can choose to put your immersive daydreaming to one side and remain grounded firmly in reality. Or you can choose to explore your talent for daydreaming and see where it can take you. You can daydream when it helps you and avoid it when it doesn't.

How to stay well

One thing you do need to do is make sure that your daydreaming never takes over again the way it did before. This book wouldn't be complete without me saying a few words about how to stay well now that you've overcome your maladaptive daydreaming.

In Chapter 3, you learned how daydreaming becomes maladaptive. And by the time you finished Chapter 8, you understood why you needed to use daydreaming to escape or to meet a need. You've seen why it's so easy to resort to daydreaming when things aren't going well. And you've realized why you became dependent on daydreaming as a coping mechanism when you didn't know any other way to cope.

KEEP CHECKING IN WITH YOURSELF

All of that knowledge will help you going forward, because in future it will be much easier for you to recognize when you're using your daydreaming in a way that's not healthy. You'll be able to spot the early signs of your daydreaming getting out of control before it starts causing serious problems in other areas of your life. But to spot those signs, you need to regularly check in with yourself.

If your daydreaming is now more immersive than maladaptive, you can stop completing the self-monitoring forms we introduced in Chapter 6. Once your daydreaming is under control, you don't need to monitor it in that much detail. But you do need to remain vigilant. Ask yourself, regularly, what you're using your daydreaming for. If it's a fun distraction when you're bored or a way to relax at the end of a day well lived, you're good. If you occasionally drop into a brief daydream to process intense emotions or allow them to pass, that's still OK. But if you're regularly using daydreaming to avoid something you know you should be dealing with, that's a warning sign. If you've understood everything that we've covered in this book, you know where the boundary is. You just have to keep being honest with yourself. And you have to keep asking the question: *"Is the way I'm daydreaming today healthy for me?"* That's a question you'll need to keep asking yourself for the rest of your life. It's the price you pay for being an immersive daydreamer.

KEEP WORKING ON REAL LIFE

The other way to stay healthy is by leaning in to the things we discussed in Chapter 9. It will *always* be easier to keep your daydreaming under control if real life isn't somewhere you need to run away from. Real life has to be somewhere you want to be, otherwise your daydreaming will always feel like the more attractive option. Make sure you're building a strong social network. Find friends who love and accept you for who you are. Find people who will support you through the tough times so that you don't have to depend on your characters. Surround yourself with people who will enrich your life through their unique perspectives and opinions in a way that characters you create never can.

Alongside building that social network, set yourself some compelling, ambitious goals, and then get excited about working toward them. Find the joy in daring to dream big and then making it happen. If you can wake up every morning eager to see what you can do with the day ahead, you won't be tempted to stay in bed and daydream. And when you achieve something awesome in real life, it will be so much more satisfying than when you daydreamed about it, precisely because of the effort you had to put into it.

YOU'VE GOT THIS

Ultimately, *you* are responsible for keeping your daydreaming under control. If your daydreaming was controlling you for a long time, it might be daunting to realize that you've turned the tables on it. It might be hard to accept that you're now in charge of that powerful force that you used to think was ruining your life. But *you* are the powerful one. *You* decided that enough was enough and that something had to change. That's why you bought this book.

In the worst-case scenario, if things go badly wrong and your daydreaming becomes maladaptive again, this book will still be here. You can work through it again. But my hope is that you won't need to. You've done the hard work this time. I hope you're seeing the results. I was your guide, but you were the one who did the work. And trust me, after doing all of that work, after beating this powerful addiction, staying well is something you're more than capable of. In fact, you're on your way to becoming that unstoppable force that your daydream self has probably been all along.

The benefits of staying well

The most compassionate and sustainable way to overcome maladaptive daydreaming is to let go of the parts of your daydreaming that made it maladaptive and embrace your abilities as an immersive daydreamer. Let's sum up one final time why that is.

The fun part is that you can keep your stories and your characters. You've probably spent a long time crafting your daydream world, and you're almost certainly emotionally attached to at least some of your characters. As an immersive daydreamer, you don't have to give that up. You keep the best parts of your daydreaming – the fun, the adventures and the connections – while giving up the harmful parts – the uncontrollable urges, the inability to stay focussed, the social isolation, the shame and all the other damaging consequences of excessive daydreaming.

You also get to keep your daydream self and, better than that, you can bring the best parts of your daydream self into your real life. Your daydreaming connects you with who you truly are at your core so that you can show up in the real world in a way that's authentic, empowering and deeply fulfilling.

When you don't need to daydream as a coping mechanism, you're free to daydream for enjoyment or to use your daydreaming to your advantage. Instead of allowing your excessive daydreaming to destroy your motivation for working on real life, you can use your talent for positive visualization to inspire you to work toward the future you want.

Moving to immersive daydreaming can also help you fall in love with your imagination. As a maladaptive daydreamer, you probably resented your imagination for being so powerful that you couldn't control it. But now, you're able to see it for the creative gift it is and hopefully even be thankful that your mind works this way.

Possibly the biggest gift that you've given yourself in overcoming your maladaptive daydreaming is that you've finally been able to release the shame you've felt for most of your life. You don't have to see yourself as defective or broken or a loser, because you aren't any of those things. You're someone who went through something difficult, and you've come out the other side stronger, happier and determined to live life to the full from this point forward. Now you know that being a daydreamer isn't weird or unhealthy or embarrassing. Everyone's mind works differently. Daydreaming happens to be the way you think. That might cause you a few problems in some areas, but it makes you incredibly talented in others. And as you start to internalize this new, more positive, mindset, any remaining shame will fall away because there will be nothing for it to hold on to.

Healing brings peace

In the years since I first heard about immersive and maladaptive daydreaming, I've been able to make peace with my daydreaming. I've accepted that my daydream world is as much a part of me as the real world. And I've been able to improve both worlds by bringing my real-life self and my daydream self closer together. In many ways, I'm a mass of contradictions. I'm insatiably curious. I have a deep need for adventure and excitement. But I also want peace and stability. I want to be always on the move, discovering new things, exploring infinite possibilities. But at the same time, I want to slow down and connect more deeply with the people I care about. No matter how much I have, I will always want more. More than anyone could possibly fit into one lifetime. And so I'm incredibly grateful that my daydreaming gives me the chance to experience *more*.

Everyone has to deal with conflicting priorities and competing desires. That's part of life. And for most people, that means deciding what's most important, building a life around that and letting the rest go. But I don't have to let anything go. I've taken the things that matter most and created a life that's happier and more fulfilling than anything I could have imagined just a few years ago. And all of those wonderful delicious maybes that don't fit into my real life go into my daydreams. One life isn't enough for me, but thanks to my wild imagination, I can have as many lives as I need.

The greatest gift my daydreaming has given me is that it brought me back to myself. Faced with expectations that didn't align with who I was, all too often I sacrificed my authenticity in order to fit in. In the real world, I'd lost touch with who I was and what I wanted from life. My daydream self helped me to recover my authenticity and, in the process, taught me that having the courage to be yourself is one of the most powerful forms of self-care.

I was born a daydreamer. I have no concept of what it's like to live in just one world. But I no longer resent that. I have meaning and purpose in my life, and I'm happy – deeply, soul-level happy. Who can ask for more than that?

YOU CAN FIND THAT PEACE TOO

I hope that as you've read this book, you've come to believe not only that you can overcome your maladaptive daydreaming but also that you can turn your huge imagination into the superpower it was always meant to be. Perhaps you've already made significant progress in your healing journey. I hope I've convinced you that healing is possible and that you already have within you all the resources you need to build the life you want to live. Because, ultimately, it's your life. You don't have to follow the suggestions in this book forever. As you come to understand yourself and your daydreaming, you'll learn to trust your instincts and you'll be able to figure out what works for you.

Let's normalize being a daydreamer

I want to end this book by reminding you of where you began. Do you remember when you felt alone? When you thought you were the only person in the world who daydreams in this way? Do you remember the relief you felt when you found out that maladaptive daydreaming is something other people do too? There are still millions of immersive and maladaptive daydreamers across the world who think it's just them. And that's a lonely place to be.

There are also far too many immersive daydreamers who've learned about maladaptive daydreaming from misinformation on the internet and now fear that their harmless fantasies constitute a serious mental-health problem.

So please, let's normalize immersive daydreaming as the beautiful creative trait that it is, while at the same time raising awareness of how damaging maladaptive daydreaming can be. Don't keep your daydreaming a secret. Allow it to come up in conversation. You don't have to shout it from the rooftops, but don't hide it either. Maladaptive daydreaming is thought to affect one person in 40. That means there's a good chance that someone you know is a maladaptive daydreamer, just like you used to be. You almost certainly don't know about it, because far too many of us don't talk about it. You can change that.

When you're open about your daydreaming, you send a signal to others that this is something it's OK to talk about. And, more importantly, when you're open about your daydreaming, you let other daydreamers know they're not alone, even if they don't choose to tell you at the time. You could change someone's life and never even realize it. So don't hide your daydreaming. And don't hide the incredible healing journey you've been on. If you've overcome maladaptive daydreaming using the strategies in this book, you should be extremely proud of yourself. You took charge of your mental health, you made a commitment to get well, and you followed through on it. That's worth celebrating!

Your daydreaming is just one part of what makes you the awesome person you are. But it's an important and special part. I hope you'll agree that it's a privilege to have a mind that works like this, that opens doors to endless possibilities. Over the coming months and years, you'll decide how you want to use your beautiful imagination to take you where you want to go, both in reality and in your daydreams. The direction you take from here will be personal to you. Your journey is just beginning. And it's going to be incredible.

RESOURCES

All the resources in this section are things that I've found helpful in my own journey of overcoming maladaptive daydreaming and learning to love my imagination.

The links in this section can also be found at https://daydreamplace.com/resources/

To learn more about maladaptive daydreaming

The best places to start are the ISMD (https://maladaptiveday dreamingsociety.com) and the ICMDR (https://daydreamresearch. wixsite.com/md-research). Many of the research articles listed in the reference list are freely available from the ICMDR website.

MALADAPTIVE DAYDREAMING ARTICLES

Jayne Bigelsen's article in *The Atlantic* was one of the first descriptions of maladaptive daydreaming written by someone with lived experience of the condition: Jayne Bigelsen and Tina Kelley. (29 April 2015). "When daydreaming replaces real life: Should elaborate fantasies be considered a psychiatric disorder?" *The Atlantic*. https://www.theatlantic.com/health/archive/2015/04/when-daydreaming-replaces-real-life/391319.

"The Secret Life of Walter Mitty" is the best-known fictional depiction of maladaptive daydreaming. The original short story captures the essential features of the condition far better than the film versions: James Thurber. (11 March 1939). "The Secret Life of Walter Mitty". *The New Yorker*. https://www.newyorker.com/magazine/1939/03/18/the-secret-life-of-walter-mitty-james-thurber.

PODCASTS AND VIDEOS ABOUT MALADAPTIVE DAYDREAMING

Parallel Lives is the main podcast specifically serving the maladaptive daydreaming community: https://www.youtube.com/channel/UCfDflux4tX-ICiMFP_U-oQg.

Maladaptive daydreaming researcher Nirit Soffer-Dudek talks about the connection between maladaptive daydreaming and ADHD in this podcast: ADDitude. (20 July 2022). "Maladaptive Daydreaming vs. ADHD: Important similarities and distinctive differences" (No. 412). ADHD Experts Podcast. https://www.additudemag.com/webinar/maladaptive-daydreaming-adhd-mind-wandering.

The Daydreamers is a short film directed by Thomas Renckens, which features two maladaptive daydreamers talking to the psychologist Professor Eli Somer: Thomas Renckens. (2020). *The Daydreamers*.

National Film and Television School. https://thomaswillemrenckens.com/THE-DAYDREAMERS.

ARTICLES TO HELP YOU EXPLAIN MALADAPTIVE DAYDREAMING

When you first talk to your doctor or to a friend or family member about maladaptive daydreaming, it can be helpful to have a brief article that explains what it is so that you don't have to. The ISMD website has two downloadable leaflets that are designed to give a brief overview of maladaptive daydreaming. They can be accessed at https://maladaptivedaydreamingsociety.com/resources/

This article published in BJGP Life would be a good article to show your doctor: Sara Noden. (13 October 2023). "Maladaptive daydreaming in general practice: An emerging challenge". BJGP Life. https://bjgplife.com/maladaptive-daydreaming.

And this article from Verywell Health is an accessible description of maladaptive daydreaming that could help you explain it to family and friends: Elizabeth Yuko. (16 November 2023). "What is maladaptive daydreaming and how can I stop it?" Verywell Health. https://www.verywellhealth.com/maladaptive-daydreaming-5194802.

Support groups

REDDIT:
For maladaptive daydreamers: r/MaladaptiveDreaming
For immersive daydreamers: r/ImmersiveDaydreaming

FACEBOOK:
Maladaptive Daydreaming Disorder Support
Maladaptive Daydreamers
Maladaptive Daydreaming: A day in the life of a dreamer

DISCORD:
Maladaptive Daydreaming: https://discord.com/invite/k6eM4PapMS

Mindfulness

Mindfulness helped me to overcome not only maladaptive daydreaming but also decades of depression. The mindfulness course that changed my life is MBCT. The similar MBSR course is freely available at the Palouse Mindfulness website: https://palousemindfulness.com.

An audio version of the three-minute breathing space introduced in Chapter 9 can be found at: Sam DC. (4 October 2016). "The Breathing Space by Jon Kabat Zinn". YouTube. https://www.youtube.com/watch?v=8oWmGJc8NWI.

This video from DBT-RU is a good introduction to present-moment awareness: DBT-RU: DBT Skills from Experts. (8 December 2020). "Mindfulness What". YouTube. https://www.youtube.com/watch?v=JUSaQL1_zXE.

Dialectical behaviour therapy

DBT teaches you to manage uncomfortable emotions. The inability to tolerate emotional discomfort is the reason many immersive daydreamers develop maladaptive daydreaming disorder. Unfortunately, DBT is not widely available and can be prohibitively expensive. The videos from DBT-RU explain the basic concepts and may help you even if you can't find a DBT therapist: https://www.youtube.com/@DBTRU.

Marsha Linehan's DBT workbook is a must-read for anyone interested in using DBT techniques: Marsha Linehan. (2014). *DBT Skills Training Handouts and Worksheets* (2nd edn.). Guilford Press.

Urge surfing (see Chapter 10) is a DBT technique. You can learn more about it in this video: Jennifer May, Ph.D. (31 May 2020). "DBT – Mindfulness – Urge Surfing". YouTube. https://www.youtube.com/watch?v=RIA2ewXayTc.

Miscellaneous good stuff

TAI CHI TO CURB MORNING DAYDREAMING

Doing 15 minutes of tai chi as soon as I wake up helps me control the urge to daydream and gets my day off to a productive start. The video I use can be found at: Pedram Shojai (taoistpathschool). (15 November 2011). "Tai Chi Qi Gong". YouTube. https://www.youtube.com/watch?v=HKI-8ZWLfyY.

PODCASTS TO KEEP YOUR MIND BUSY

Podcasts are my go-to method of getting mundane tasks done without daydreaming. They're also a great substitute for music if you need to reduce how much music you listen to while you get your daydreaming under control. My personal favourite is the Mel Robbins podcast, which is easy and fun to listen to and also boosts your motivation to work on real life: https://www.melrobbins.com/podcast.

The Daydream Place

Lastly, if you want to continue your connection with me, check out my website: https://daydreamplace.com/. I blog every week about various aspects of immersive and maladaptive daydreaming. Alternatively, you can connect with me on Instagram at: kyla_m_dreams.

REFERENCE LIST

American Psychiatric Association. (2022). *Diagnostic and Statistical Manual of Mental Disorders* (5th edn., text rev.). https://doi.org/10.1176/appi.books.9780890425787.

Burton, N. (2 March 2012). "The Anatomy of Melancholy – Can Depression Be Good for You?" TEDx Talks. [Video]. YouTube. https://www.youtube.com/watch?v=ndsB37KUAso.

Herscu, O. (2021). "Treatment for Maladaptive Daydreaming: A pioneering study on the development and evaluation of an online intervention based on mindfulness meditation and self-monitoring". Doctoral dissertation presented to the School of Social Work, University of Haifa, Israel (in Hebrew, English abstract).

Herscu, O., Somer, E., Federman, A., Soffer-Dudek, N. (2023). "Mindfulness meditation and self-monitoring reduced maladaptive daydreaming symptoms: A randomized controlled trial of a brief self-guided web-based program". *Journal of Consulting and Clinical Psychology*, 91(5), 285–300. https://doi.org/10.1037/ccp0000790.

Killingsworth, M. A., Gilbert, D. T. (2010). "A wandering mind is an unhappy mind". *Science*, 330(6006): 932. https://www.science.org/doi/10.1126/science.1192439.

Maté, G. (2018). *In the Realm of Hungry Ghosts: Close encounters with addiction*. Penguin Random House UK, London. p. 37.

Maté, G. (2022). *The Myth of Normal: Trauma, illness and healing in a toxic culture*. Vermilion, London, p. 224.

Ross, C. A., West, M., Somer, E. (2020). "Self-reported medication and recreational drug effectiveness in maladaptive daydreaming".

Journal of Nervous and Mental Disease, 208(1), 77–80. https://doi.org/10.1097/nmd.0000000000001091.

Soffer-Dudek, N., Theodor-Katz, N. (2022). "Maladaptive daydreaming: Epidemiological data on a newly identified syndrome". *Frontiers in Psychiatry*, 13, 871041. https://doi.org/10.3389/fpsyt.2022.871041.

Somer, E. (2002). "Maladaptive daydreaming: A qualitative inquiry". *Journal of Contemporary Psychotherapy*, 32(2), 195–210. https://doi.org/10.1023/A:1020597026919.

Somer, E., Somer, L., Jopp, S. D. (2016a). "Childhood antecedents and maintaining factors in maladaptive daydreaming". *Journal of Nervous and Mental Disease*, 204(6), 471–478. http://dx.doi.org/10.1097/NMD.0000000000000507.

Somer, E., Somer, L., Jopp, S. D. (2016b). "Parallel lives: A phenomenological study of the lived experience of maladaptive daydreaming". *Journal of Trauma and Dissociation*, 17(5), 561–576. http://dx.doi.org/10.1080/15299732.2016.1160463.

Somer, E., Soffer-Dudek, N., Ross, C. A. (2017a). "The comorbidity of daydreaming disorder (maladaptive daydreaming)". *Journal of Nervous and Mental Disease*, 205(7), 525–530. http://dx.doi.org/10.1097/NMD.0000000000000685.

Somer, E., Soffer-Dudek, N., Ross, C. A., Halpern, N. (2017b). "Maladaptive daydreaming: Proposed diagnostic criteria and their assessment with a structured clinical interview". *Psychology of Consciousness: Theory, Research, and Practice*, 4(2), 176-189. http://dx.doi.org/10.1037/cns0000114.

Somer, E., Abu-Rayya, H. M., Brenner, R. (2021). "Childhood trauma and maladaptive daydreaming: Fantasy functions and themes in a multi-country sample". *Journal of Trauma & Dissociation: The official journal of the International Society for the Study of Dissociation*, 22(3), 288–303. https://doi.org/10.1080/15299732.2020.1809599.

Taylor, M., Hodges, S. D., Kohányi, A. (2003). "The illusion of independent agency: Do adult fiction writers experience their characters as having minds of their own?" *Imagination, Cognition and Personality*, 22(4), 361–380. https://doi.org/10.2190/FTG3-Q9T0-7U26-5Q5X.

Theodor-Katz, N., Somer, E., Hesseg, R. M., Soffer-Dudek, N. (2022). "Could immersive daydreaming underlie a deficit in attention? The prevalence and characteristics of maladaptive daydreaming in individuals with attention-deficit/hyperactivity disorder". *Journal of Clinical Psychology*, 78, 2309-2328. https://doi.org/10.1002/jclp.23355.

ACKNOWLEDGEMENTS

Thanks go to my developmental editor, Melissa Kirk, for helping me shape my first draft into something publishable. Without her input, I suspect most of my readers wouldn't have made it past the end of Chapter 3. Thank you also to Soraya Nair, Tess Jolly and the rest of the team at Cherish who have worked so hard to bring this book into the world, helping me to fulfil a lifelong dream in the process.

I am forever grateful to my husband, Mike, and our three children. Writing a book is a far bigger undertaking than I realized, and without their love and support I don't think I would have seen it through to the end.

I also need to thank all of the staff at the Priory Hospital North London for putting me back together after my breakdown, and my fellow patients for so courageously demonstrating what it means to be authentically and vulnerably human. The month I spent with you profoundly changed me in ways that I'm grateful for each and every day. Thank you also to my therapist, who continues to provide a safe space where I can untangle my thoughts and grow into the person I was always meant to be.

Finally, and perhaps most importantly, I'd like to thank the maladaptive daydreamers who bravely allowed me to use their stories in this book. In most cases I have used pseudonyms to ensure anonymity, but Sola and Chet asked to appear under their real names. All expressed the hope that by sharing their experience, they will enable other maladaptive daydreamers to feel seen and understood. I am also grateful to the countless maladaptive daydreamers who have participated in online support groups, particularly the r/MaladaptiveDreaming subreddit. You have helped me better understand the wide range of challenges faced by those suffering from maladaptive daydreaming. I wish you all well.

AUTHOR BIOGRAPHY

Kyla Borcherds is a writer, mum, mental-health geek and lifelong daydreamer. In 2018, she learned that the "stories in her head" had a name – maladaptive daydreaming. And that started her on a quest to understand and tame her vivid imagination. In healing from maladaptive daydreaming, she discovered the importance of overcoming shame, confronting trauma and reconnecting with her authentic self. She reinvented herself, overcame decades of depression and turned her daydreaming from a damaging addiction into a powerful tool for self-development. She is now committed to helping other maladaptive daydreamers do the same.

Kyla is a prominent member of the maladaptive daydreaming community and the author of The Daydream Place, one of the largest blogs devoted to immersive and maladaptive daydreaming.

Kyla left a lengthy publishing career in 2021 to focus full-time on her writing. She lives in Birmingham, UK, with her husband, children and a few very special fictional characters.

ABOUT CHERISH EDITIONS

Cherish Editions is a bespoke publishing service for authors of mental health, wellbeing and inspirational books.

As a division of Trigger Publishing, the UK's leading independent mental health and wellbeing publisher, we are experienced in creating and selling positive, responsible, important and inspirational books, which work to de-stigmatize the issues around mental health and improve the mental health and wellbeing of those who read our titles.

Founded by Adam Shaw, a mental health advocate, author and philanthropist, and leading psychologist Lauren Callaghan, Cherish Editions aims to publish books that provide advice, support and inspiration. We nurture our authors so that their stories can unfurl on the page, helping them to share their uplifting and moving stories.

Cherish Editions is unique in that a percentage of the profits from the sale of our books goes directly to leading mental health charity Shawmind, to deliver its vision to provide support for those experiencing mental ill health.

Find out more about Cherish Editions by visiting cherisheditions.com or joining us on:
Twitter @cherisheditions
Facebook @cherisheditions
Instagram @cherisheditions

Cherish
EDITIONS

ABOUT SHAWMIND

A proportion of profits from the sale of all Trigger books go to their sister charity, Shawmind, also founded by Adam Shaw and Lauren Callaghan. The charity aims to ensure that everyone has access to mental health resources whenever they need them.

Find out more about the work Shawmind do by visiting shawmind.org or joining them on:
  Twitter @Shawmind_
  Facebook @ShawmindUK
  Instagram @Shawmind_

Shawmind
Your Local Mental Health & Wellbeing Charity

Milton Keynes UK
Ingram Content Group UK Ltd.
UKHW022127201024
449871UK00009B/39

9 781916 920644